Sylvan Barnet

Morton Berman

William Burto

INSTRUCTOR'S MANUAL TO ACCOMPANY

AN INTRODUCTION TO

LITERATURE

Fiction / Poetry / Drama

Seventh Edition

Little, Brown and Company

Boston   Toronto

ISBN 0-316-082120

9 8 7 6 5 4 3 2 1

SEM

Published simultaneously in Canada by Little, Brown & Company (Canada) Limited

Printed in the United States of America

ACKNOWLEDGMENTS

Paul Dehn. "O Nuclear Wind" from *Quake, Quake, Quake* by Paul Dehn. Copyright 1958, 1961 by Paul Dehn. Reprinted by permission of Simon and Schuster.

Robert Frost. "In White," contained in a letter from Robert Frost to Susan Ward, January 15, 1912 (HM 25361), is reproduced by permission of The Huntington Library, San Marino, California.

William Butler Yeats. Lines from "The Man and the Echo" in *Collected Poems* by William Butler Yeats are reprinted with permission of Macmillan Publishing Co., Inc. and Gage Publishing Ltd. Copyright 1940 by Georgie Yeats, renewed 1968 by Bertha Georgie Yeats, Michael Butler Yeats, and Anne Yeats.

PREFACE

What follows is something close to a slightly organized card
file. In the course of writing and then of teaching *An Introduction to Literature*, we have amassed jottings of various
sorts, and these may be of some use to others as well as to
ourselves. Perhaps most useful will be the references to
critical articles and books that we have profited from. We
have plowed through a fair amount of material and tried to
call attention to some of the best. We have also offered suggestions for theme assignments, but many of the questions
printed at the ends of sections in *An Introduction to Literature* are suitable topics for writing. We have offered, too,
relatively detailed comment on some of the stories, poems, and
plays. (Most of the comments on *The Misanthrope*, *Death of a
Salesman*, and *Equus* are drawn from our *Types of Drama*; the
comments on *Ivan Ilych* and *The Metamorphosis* are drawn from
our *Nine Modern Classics*.) These may serve, especially if
they seem wrongheaded, to give an instructor a jumping-off
place.

A plaintive postscript: At the end of *An Introduction to Literature* a questionnaire invites students to offer their opin-
ions. Readers of earlier editions often told us that the book
has no light or pleasant pieces. We don't include many light
things, but there are some, and on checking with instructors
we found that the lighter pieces were rarely assigned. If
your students have grumbled that writers always seem to be
talking about unhappy love affairs and death, you may want to
assign some of the following pieces: Thurber's "The Secret
Life of Walter Mitty," Donald Barthelme's "The School," Toni
Cade Bambara's "The Lesson"; X. J. Kennedy's "In a Prominent
Bar in Secaucus One Day," the anonymous "My Sweetheart's the
Mule in the Mines," Burns's "Mary Morrison," Cummings's "next
to of course god amierca i," Updike's "Youth's Progress,"
Dorothy Parker's "Indian Summer," Burns's "A Red, Red Rose,"
Waller's "Song," Frost's "The Pasture," Pound's "An Immorality,"
William Carlos Williams's "The Dance" and "This Is Just to Say,"
Robert Francis's "The Pitcher," George Starbuck's "Fable for
Blackboard," Herrick's "Corinna's Going A-Maying," Wordsworth's
"I Wandered Lonely as a Cloud," and Anthony Hecht's "The Dover
Bitch."

CONTENTS

THE FIRST MEETING

The night before the first class, every teacher knows the
truth of Byron's observation: "Nothing so difficult as a beginning." What to do in the first meeting is always worrisome.
Students will not, of course, have prepared anything, and you
can't say, "Let's open the book to page such-and-such," because half of them won't have the book. How, then, can one
use the time profitably? A friend of ours (Marcia Stubbs, of
Wellesley College) offers a suggestion. We have tried it and
we know it works, so we suggest that you consider it, too, if
you are looking for an interesting beginning.

Begin reading the Japanese anecdote (page 15) aloud, stopping
after "A heavy rain was still falling." Then ask, "What do
you think will happen now?" Someone is bound to volunteer
"They'll meet someone." Whom will they meet? (It may be
necessary to say at this point that Tanzan and Ekido are both
men.) You will certainly be informed that if two men meet
someone, it will be a woman. Continue reading "Coming around
the bend they met a lovely girl. . . ." After "unable to
cross the intersection," ask again what will happen, and enter-
tain answers until you get an appropriate response. Read
again, and pause after "temple." Who are Tanzan and Ekido?
The temple may suggest to someone that they are monks; if not,
provide the information. Continue reading, up through "Why
did you do that?" Now inform the class that the story ends
with one more line of print, and ask them to supply the brief
ending. It is unlikely that anyone will come close. Read the
ending. The students will then see the perfect rightness of
it.

The point of the exercise: First, a story sets up expectations,
partly by *excluding* possibilities. (A relevant remark by
Robert Frost appears on page 425, but it can be effectively
introduced at the first meeting. A work of literature --
Frost is talking about a poem, but we can generalize --
"assumes direction with the first line laid down.") After the
first line or so the possibilities are finite. The story must
go on to fulfill the expectations set up. At the same time,

1

a story, to be entertaining, must surprise us by taking us beyond what we have imagined and expect. But the fulfillment and the surprise must be coherent or the story teller will appear arbitrary and the story, no matter how entertaining, trivial. (Notice E. M. Forster's pertinent comment, quoted on page 20: "Shock, followed by the feeling, 'Oh, that's all right,' is a sign that all is well with the plot.") By satisfying expectations literature confirms the truth of our own experience, teaching us that we are not alone, not singular; our perceptions, including moral perceptions (e.g., cause leads to effect, guilt leads to punishment or retribution) are shared by other human beings, people who may not even be of our own century or culture. Something along these lines can be suggested at the first meeting; subsequent meetings can be devoted to showing that literature, by exceeding and yet not violating our expectations, can also expand our powers of observation, imagination, and judgment.

SOME THEORIES OF LITERATURE

Most of this material is sufficiently new to students that the instructors may find they must say it all over again if the students are to understand it. Examples from painting and sculpture usually help to make the imitative theory clear, and students then see its relevance to film and drama. The expressive theory is probably closer to their hearts, especially because they commonly believe a writer must "be sincere." A mischievous instructor might tell them what Ezra Pound said of sincerity in *The Paris Review* 28 (1962), p. 25: "Technique is the test of sincerity. If a thing isn't worth getting the technique to say, it is of inferior value." But one must then go into technique. W. K. Wimsatt, Jr., and Monroe Beardsley's famous "The Intentional Fallacy," in Wimsatt's *The Verbal Icon*, is, of course, a subtle examination of one aspect of the expressive theory; Wimsatt and Beardsley's "Affective Fallacy" (again in Wimsatt's book) is an equally subtle analysis of one aspect of the affective theory. Beardsley, in *Aesthetics*, refines his earlier arguments, and Wimsatt does likewise in an essay in *The Discipline of Criticism*, edited by Peter Demetz et al.

A related question is: Does literature *do* anything? Does it shape character, does it move men to action? Persons who wish to ban books pay them the compliment of assuming that books can have an effect on readers. In "The Man and the Echo" W. B. Yeats asks such questions but leaves them unresolved: did some of his poems and plays cause Irish patriots to be killed by the English during the Easter Rebellion of 1916?

> All that I have said and done,
> Now that I am old and ill,
> Turns into a question till
> I lie awake night after night
> And never get the answers right.
> Did that play of mine send out
> Certain men the English shot?
> Did words of mine put too great strain
> On that woman's reeling brain?

Could my spoken words have checked
That whereby a house lay wrecked?

Toni Cade Bambara's story, "The Lesson," is in its amusing way revolutionary, and might well be taught along with this chapter.

Instructors will probably find that students are eager to say that literature gives knowledge about people. A little probing (Why not stick to history's account of Julius Caesar, and forget Shakespeare's?) will probably get responses that the instructor can help shape into more thoughtful statements about literature. Finally, although some of our colleagues prefer to postpone teaching this chapter until students have read several short stories, we have found that college freshmen have read enough to discuss the problem if in high school they have read a couple of novels and stories and a play by Shakespeare. Also some pieces in *An Introduction to Literature* -- notably Archibald MacLeish's "Ars Poetica" and Marianne Moore's "Poetry" -- inevitably arouse discussion about the nature of art; MacLeish's poem is probably the easiest to handle at this stage.

4

STORIES AND MEANINGS

Parables vary in the amount of allegory they contain. In the
Parable of the Good Samaritan, the man who fell among thieves
has no equivalent -- he is what he is, an unfortunate man --
nor do the thieves. And the priest and the Levite are indistinguishable; both are, let us say, unloving men or men without fellow-feeling, whereas the Samaritan is a man with fellow-
feeling. Our point is that in a parable there is *some* allegory -- some equivalent -- but there may also be some material
necessary to the story that has no equivalent. A parable
usually does not have the systematic equivalents of, say, this
allegorical poem by Sir Walter Raleigh:

> What is our life? A play of passion,
> Our mirth the music of division.
> Our mothers' wombs the tiring-houses be,
> Where we are dressed for this short comedy.
> Heaven the judicious sharp spectator is,
> That sits and marks still who doth act amiss.
> Our graves that hide us from the searching sun
> Are like drawn curtains when the play is done.
> Thus march we, playing, to our latest rest,
> Only we die in earnest, that's no jest.

Luke, "Parable of the Good Samaritan" (Luke 10:30-37). G. B.
Caird, in *The Pelican Gospel Commentaries: The Gospel of St.
Luke*, suggests that this parable "perfectly illustrates the
difference between the ethics of law and the ethics of love."
Caird goes on to say that Jesus tells the story of the Good
Samaritan "not to answer the question 'Who is my neighbor?'
but to show that it is the wrong question. The proper question is, 'To whom can I be a neighbor?'; and the answer is,
'To anyone whose need constitutes a claim on my love.'"
Another point: In Old Testament times, and in Christ's day,
the Samaritans (who lived in what is now western Jordan) took
as their code the Pentateuch (the five books of Moses) and
claimed to be Israelites, but the Jews rejected the Samaritans,
regarding them as transplanted Assyrians. In the parable,

presumably the man who "went down from Jerusalem to Jericho" (a trip of seventeen miles) was a Jew, and we might reasonably expect the priest and the Levite (one of the tribe of Levi, assistants to the Temple priests) to assist their countryman and coreligionist. But these two avoid him, and, surprisingly, aid comes from a foreign traveler, a traditional enemy.

Petronius, "The Widow of Ephesus." This story is a gem, and perhaps it is a shame to throw it away in a discussion that is intended to give the students some critical vocabulary. Still, they ought to admire it more if they look closely at it, and notice (for example) that the dialogue begins not with the soldier but with the maid. We are told that the soldier spoke to the lady, and the gist of his arguments is presented, but presumably he is not at first especially successful, and so we get a report (or a *summary*) rather than the vivid dialogue of a dramatized *scene*. The maid's words, and of course the soldier's looks, persuade the lady: without the maid, the lady would seem grossly indecent. And at the end, when the lady must act to save her lover, we get dialogue. Her decision to put the body of her husband on the cross is given in her own words, prefaced by the narrator's ironic statement that the lady was no less tender than pure. The last sentence of the story is a brief, understated, ironic report of the townspeople's reaction. For an interesting discussion of sources and analogues (though not much suited to class use), see Allen Cabaniss, *Liturgy and Literature*. Cabaniss points out that in the version attributed to Phaedrus (A.D. 14?-66?), the maid is incidental; the widow was famous only for her fidelity to her dead husband, the soldier is thirsty and asks the maid for water (rather than seeing a strange light and hearing groans, and therefore going to investigate), and near the end he is troubled by the loss of the body but does not think of suicide and interment next to the husband. Another highly interesting essay (though not especially useful in teaching this story in an introductory course) is Peter Ure's survey of the many variations of this tale over the centuries. Ure's essay is in his *Elizabethan and Jacobean Drama*.

Luke, "Parable of the Prodigal Son" (Luke 15:11-32). G. B. Caird points out (in his *Pelican Gospel Commentaries: The Gospel of St. Luke*) that the traditional title "does less than justice to the purpose of the parable, as the opening sentence makes clear. 'There was a man who had two sons,' and he lost both of them, one in a foreign country, the other behind a barricade of self-righteousness. The elder contrived, without leaving home, to be as far away from his father as ever his

brother was in the heathen pigsty." The selfishness of the
younger brother, Caird goes on to point out, was a reckless
love of the world, that of the elder brother was (despite his
obedience) a cold self-centeredness. Notice that we are not
told by the speaker of the parable how the younger brother
squandered his fortune, other than that he squandered it in
"riotous living," which might mean mere extravagance; the
statement that it was squandered on harlots is uttered by the
elder brother. Notice, too, that the father shows "compassion"
even before the younger son expresses contrition, and that
this compassion makes unnecessary the completion of the younger
son's prepared speech. They "make merry," the younger son thus
finding at home what he had sought elsewhere. Caird points
out, too, that the father counters the cold elder son's recrim-
inations not by taking sides but by expressing love for both
sons, substituting "this thy brother" for the elder son's cold
"this thy son."

Kate Chopin, "The Story of an Hour." The first sentence of
course proves to be essential to the end of the story, though
during the middle of the story the initial care to protect
Mrs. Mallard from the "sad message" seems almost comic. Students may assume, too easily, that Mrs. Mallard's "storm of
grief" is hypocritical; and they may not notice that her renewal after the first shock is stimulated by the renewal of
life around her ("the tops of trees . . . were all aquiver
with the new spring of life"), and that before she achieves a
new life Mrs. Mallard (like the Widow of Ephesus) first goes
through a sort of death and then tries to resist renewal: her
expression "indicated a suspension of intelligent thought,"
she felt something "creeping out of the sky," and she tried to
"beat it back with her will," but she soon finds herself
"drinking the elixir of life through that open window," and
her thoughts turn to "spring days, and summer days." (Students might be invited to compare Lawrence's "The Horse Dealer's
Daughter.") The story has two surprises; the change from
grief to joy proves not to be the whole story, for we get the
second surprise, the husband's return and Mrs. Mallard's death.
The last line ("the doctors . . . said she had died . . . of
joy that kills") is doubly ironic: the doctors wrongly assume
that she was overjoyed to find that her husband was alive, but
they are not wholly wrong in guessing that her last day of
life brought her great joy. See the essay pp. 1138-1140.

Instructors frequently assign Chapters 2 and 3 as a single
assignment and spend some time on the significance of point of
view. Among stories in other chapters that go well with Chapter 2 is Lawrence's "The Horse Dealer's Daughter"; if one is

7

willing to get into a discussion of symbolism here, Lawrence's story of a woman's movement from death-in-life to renewal through love (and of Fergusson's discovery of love) can be nicely compared to Petronius's story and to Chopin's "The Story of an Hour." Some instructors assign Jackson's "The Lottery," taking it as a parable, but, as we mention in our comment in this manual, we are not convinced that "The Lottery" has a meaning, and so we do not assign it in connection with this chapter. If you want to go beyond this chapter, we suggest that you assign Jean Rhys's very short ghost story, "I Used to Live Here Once," which can be read aloud in a couple of minutes in class. As our discussion in this manual suggests (p. 27), it can be used, along with a parable, to illustrate the range of storytelling, from an emphasis on meaning to (at the other extreme) an emphasis on sheer experience.

3

NARRATIVE POINT OF VIEW

A good deal of critical discussion about point of view is in Wayne Booth, *The Rhetoric of Fiction*; for a thorough history and analysis of the concept, consult Norman Friedman, "Point of View in Fiction," *PMLA* 70 (December 1955), pp. 1160-84. Also of interest is Patrick Cruttwell, "Makers and Persons," *Hudson Review* 12 (Winter 1959-60), pp. 487-507. Among the stories in the "Collection" that go well with O'Connor's first-person "Guests of the Nation" are Hawthorne's "Young Goodman Brown" (limited omniscient) and Katherine Anne Porter's "The Jilting of Granny Weatherall" (stream of consciousness). Lawrence's "The Horse Dealer's Daughter" is relevant too, and because it is highly symbolic it can provide a transition to the next chapter. Its movement from a fairly objective pre-sentation of the family to Mabel's consciousness and then to Dr. Fergusson's consciousness approximately parallels a move-ment from apparent realism to symbolism, though of course even the early realistic details are radiant.

Frank O'Connor, "Guests of the Nation." Incidentally, the last time that we taught this story we began the hour by asking, "What is this story about?" The first answer, "War," brought the reply, "Yes, but what about war? Is it, for example, about the heroism that war sometimes stimulates?" Another student replied, "No, it's about the cruelty of war." Our point: though it is obvious to all instructors that the story is Bonaparte's, specifically about Bonaparte's growing up or initiation or movement from innocence to experience, this move-ment is not so evident to inexperienced readers.

In a sense, Jeremiah Donovan, though he thinks of himself as experienced, seems never to have grown up, never to have come to any sorrowful awareness of man's loneliness. The bickering between Noble and Hawkins is, however, not a sign of enmity but a sort of bond. They may quarrel, but at least they share a relationship. Hawkins's offer to join the Irish cause indi-cates not so much his cowardice as his intuitive awareness that life and fellowship are more important than blind nation-alism that excuses murder by an appeal to "duty."

Suggested Topic for Writing:

Question 5 lends itself well to a theme. She is a "simple
. . . countrywoman," but she knows (as the narrator finds out)
that "nothing but sorrow and want can follow the people that
disturb the hidden powers." An interview with O'Connor in
Writers at Work, Malcolm Cowley, ed. reveals some of O'Connor's
ideas about fiction. Asked why he chose the short story as
his medium, O'Connor said, "Because it's the nearest thing I
know to lyric poetry. . . . A novel actually requires far more
logic and far more knowledge of circumstances, whereas a short
story can have the sort of detachment from circumstances that
lyric poetry has." O'Connor's ideas about the short story are
expressed at some length in his book on the topic, *The Lonely
Voice.*

NOTE: Among other first-person narratives in the book are Poe,
"The Cask of Amontillado," Gilman, "The Yellow Wallpaper,"
Joyce, "Araby," Faulkner, "A Rose for Emily," Barthelme, "The
School," Updike "A&P," and Bambara, "The Lesson."

10

4

ALLEGORY AND SYMBOLISM

"Allegory" and "symbolism" have accumulated a good many meanings. Among the references to consult are Edwin Honig, *The Dark Conceit*; C. S. Lewis, *The Allegory of Love*; and Dorothy Sayers, *The Poetry of Search*. For an allegorical poem, see p. 5 of this manual. Faulkner's own reference to symbols in "The Bear" is half-joking but is not to be dismissed as a mere joke.

<u>William Faulkner, "The Bear."</u> We have sometimes begun the class hour not by turning immediately to "The Bear" but by reading aloud -- two or three times -- a short symbolic poem such as Blake's "The Sick Rose" (p. 438) or Hopkins's "Spring and Fall" (p. 416). "Spring and Fall" works especially well because -- no matter what the season when one happens to be teaching -- one can begin by talking about the symbolic implications of the season and can then turn to the poem. Then, after the students have seen that literature includes (in Henry James's words) "objects casting . . . far behind them a shadow more curious . . . than the apparent figure," one can turn to the longer work at hand.

"The Bear" will keep an instructor busy during the class hour (especially because of Faulkner's somewhat exasperating use of Keats's "Grecian Urn," which has its own problems), but one may wish to assign Lawrence's "The Horse Dealer's Daughter" or Hawthorne's "Young Goodman Brown" for the same class, and one may wish to refer ambitious students to the longer version of "The Bear" in *Go Down, Moses*.

Suggested Topics for Writing:

1. Question 2 (on the distinction between being scared and afraid) can produce good essays if students are cautioned to keep their eye on the story and not to define the words out of context.
2. What does the bear stand for? (Students should be cautioned to discuss the text of the story, and not Faulkner's comments about it.

3. Trace the development of the boy's awareness of the significance of the hunt.

STYLE

There is a good deal of subtle discussion of style in Monroe Beardsley, *Aesthetics*. Also of interest are White's chapter on style in William Strunk, Jr., and E. B. White, *The Elements of Style*, and F. L. Lucas, *Style*. And of course useful discussions are in many freshman rhetoric texts.

Ernest Hemingway, "A Clean, Well-Lighted Place." We put this story in our chapter on "Style" because it is so notable an example of the fusion of style and meaning. We think of Cardinal Newman's famous remark on style: "Thought and meaning are inseparable from each other. Matter and expression are parts of one: style is a thinking out into language."

Hemingway's style is spare because the world he sees (so different from Faulkner's rich, fertile, vibrant world) is a world of *nada*, nothing, meaninglessness. The best that this world can offer is the sympathetic understanding that one person (the older waiter) has for another who with despair perceives nada; that's why the older waiter tries to maintain "a clean, well-lighted place." (God once said, "Let there be light," but for Hemingway man has to make what light -- order -- there is.) This waiter, in contrast to the young waiter (whose unthinking confidence prevents him from understanding the old man's despair), realizes that there are people who "need" a clean, well-lighted café, hence he is reluctant to close up for the night. (Notice, too, that he specifies that "this old man is clean.") And there is, of course, a second, related, reason for his reluctance; he himself needs such a place, as is evident when he goes to the coffee bar, thus more or less repeating the old man's visit to the café.

Two other points: (1) Some readers have been puzzled by the opening dialogue. It seems clear to us that the first line is spoken by the older waiter, and (of course) the subsequent lines alternate. This means that the last line of this passage, "He has plenty of money," is spoken by the older waiter, although one might at first think that such a remark is out of

character -- as we come to perceive the character later. But
surely the point is that when the younger waiter doesn't grasp
the older waiter's special meaning of "nothing" (emptiness),
the older waiter then offers a simple explanation that the in-
sensitive younger waiter can comprehend. (2) Though we call
Hemingway's style "spare," and it is often thought of as
simple and realistic, of course it is artful, and sometimes it
is patently unnatural: "I am of those who like to stay late at
the café." Obviously Hemingway is trying to give us something
of a sense of people speaking Spanish -- but we might also say
he sets his story in Spain because he wants to be able to
quote some dialogue that has an air of formality.

"Araby" is a second story that might be assigned if one wishes
to push further the discussion of style. Students can be
asked to point out the range of styles. With very little assistance they ought to be able to hear the opulence in "the syllables of the word *Araby* were called to me through the silence
in which my soul luxuriated and cast an Eastern enchantment
over me." A moment later we hear a very different voice: "I
watched my master's face pass from amiability to sternness; he
hoped I was not beginning to idle."

A COLLECTION OF SHORT FICTION

Nathaniel Hawthorne, "Young Goodman Brown." The journey into
the forest at night (away from the town, and from daylight)
suggests, of course, a journey into the dark regions of the
self. The many ambiguities have engendered much comment in
learned journals, some of which has been reprinted in a casebook on the story, edited by Thomas Connolly. Is the ribbon
merely a part of a dream? Does Faith resist the tempter?
Does Goodman (i.e., Mister) Brown make a journey or only dream
that he makes a journey? Is the story about awareness of evil,
or is it about the crushing weight of needlessly assumed
guilt? That is, is the story about a loss of faith (Austin
Warren, in *Nathaniel Hawthorne*, says it is about "the devas-
tating effect of moral skepticism"), or is it about a religious
faith that kills one's joy in life? And of course the story
may be about loss of faith not in Christ but in human beings;
young Goodman Brown perceives his own corruption and loses
faith in mankind.

With a little warning the student can be made to see that the
characters and experiences cannot be neatly pigeonholed. For
example, it is not certain whether or not Faith yields to "the
wicked one," and, indeed, it is not certain that Brown actually
journeyed into the wood. Among the ambiguities are: (1) Do
the events occur, or are they a dream? (2) Brown calls to his
wife Faith, "look up to heaven, and resist the evil one." Has
he resisted? Apparently he is not saved -- but neither is he
lost, for he lives a long life with his wife Faith. Richard H.
Fogle points out (*New England Quarterly* 18 [December 1945],
pp. 448-65, reprinted in his *Hawthorne's Fiction*) that "ambiguity is the very essence of Hawthorne's tale." Among other
interesting critical pieces on "Young Goodman Brown" are Marius
Bewley, *The Complex Fate*; Thomas Connolly, "Hawthorne's 'Young
Goodman Brown': An Attack on Puritanic Calvinism," *American
Literature* 28 (November 1956), pp. 370-75; and Frederick C.
Crews, *The Sins of the Fathers: Hawthorne's Psychological
Themes.* Connolly argues that Brown does not lose his faith,
but rather that his faith is purified by his loss of belief
that he is of the elect. Before the journey into the woods,

he believed that man is depraved but that *he* was of the elect
and would be saved. In the forest he sees "a black mass of
cloud" hide "the brightening stars," and (according to Connolly) Brown's faith is purified, for he comes to see that he
is not different from the rest of the congregation.

Suggested Topics for Writing:

1. Ambiguity in "Young Goodman Brown."
2. Trace the stages of Brown's disillusionment.

<u>Nathaniel Hawthorne</u>, "Roger Malvin's Burial." The story ends
piously, with the assertion that with Reuben Bourne's tears
his "sin was expiated." But what was his sin? Critics have
suggested the following: desertion of Roger Malvin; failure to
bury Roger; the killing of the son; failure to be honest with
Dorcas. But surely Reuben is not guilty of Roger's death, and
his slaughter of his son is accidental. Or is it? Frederick
Crews, in a long discussion in *PMLA* 79 (1964), reprinted in
his *The Sins of the Fathers*, argues that the hunting accident
"is a sacrificial murder dictated by Reuben's unconscious
charge of patricide and by his inability to bring the charge
directly against himself." Crews insists that critics have
failed to recognize the "difference between the feeling of
guilt and the state of being guilty." Thus, Reuben may indeed be innocent of Roger's death and yet he may *feel* guilty
about that death. Hawthorne's concern, Crews argues, is "*only*
with subjective guilt as Reuben's conscience manufactures it,
independently of the moral 'sinfulness' or 'innocence' of his
outward deeds." After all, Reuben can scarcely have expiated
a sin by killing his son; rather, Crews says, he has gotten
rid of his feeling of guilt. Thus, Reuben's own belief that
"a supernatural power" guided his steps is, in Crews's word,
a "delusion." What caused his feeling of guilt? Not his desertion of Roger but his *thoughts* of deserting Roger even before he actually does so: "Nor can it be affirmed," Hawthorne
writes early in the story, "that no selfish feeling strove to
enter Reuben's heart, though the consciousness made him more
strongly resist his companion's entreaties." Crews recognizes
that there are two objections to his belief that the shooting
of the son is not accidental: (1) Reuben fires at an unseen
target, and (2) God may be responsible for the deed. Crews
replies, first, that although Reuben certainly is not conscious
that he is shooting his son, his *un*conscious mind is guiding
him; second, Hawthorne's assertion that Reuben "believed that
a supernatural voice called him on" clearly alerts us to think
of another explanation. Crews's entire discussion of the story
is highly recommended.

Edgar Allen Poe, "The Cask of Amontillado." It may be well to
begin a class discussion by asking the students to characterize
the narrator. The opening paragraph itself, if read aloud in
class, ought to provide enough for them to see that the speaker
probably is paranoid and is given to a sort of monstrous rea-
soning, though of course at the start of the story we cannot
be absolutely certain that Fortunato has not indeed heaped a
"thousand injuries" on him. (In this paragraph, notice too
the word "impunity," which we later learn is part of the family
motto.) When we meet Fortunato, we are convinced that though
the narrator's enemy is something of a fool, he is not the
monster that the narrator thinks Fortunato is. And so the
words at the end of the story, fifty years later, must have an
ironic tone, for though *In pace requiescat* can apply to Fortunato, they cannot apply to the speaker, who is still talking
of his vengeance on the unfortunate Fortunato.

The story is full of other little ironies: the narrator is
courteous but murderous; the time is one of festivity but a
murder is being planned; the festival of disguise corresponds
to the narrator's disguise of his feelings; Fortunato thinks
he is festively disguised as a fool, but he *is* a fool; he says
he will not die of a cough, and the narrator assures him that
he is right; Fortunato is a freemason, and when he asks the
narrator for the secret sign of a brother, the narrator boldly,
playfully, outrageously shows him the mason's trowel which
soon will be used to wall Fortunato up. But what to make out
of all this? It has been the fashion, for at least a few
decades, to say that Poe's situations and themes speak to our
anxieties, our fear of being buried alive, our fear of disin-
tegration of the self, etc. Maybe. Maybe, too, there is
something to Marie Bonaparte's interpretation; she sees the
journey through the tunnel to the crypt as an entry into the
womb; the narrator is killing his father (Fortunato) and
possessing his mother. And maybe, too, there is something to
Daniel Hoffman's assertion in *Poe Poe Poe Poe Poe Poe Poe*
(p. 223) that Mon*tresor* and *Fortun*ato are doubles: "When Mon-
tresor leads Fortunato down into the farthest vault of his
family's wine-cellar, into a catacomb of human bones, is he
not . . . conducting his double thither? My treasure, my fortune, down into the bowels of the earth, a charnel-house of
bones." Maybe.

Leo Tolstoy, "The Death of Ivan Ilych." (The following discussion reprints an afterword in our *Nine Modern Classics: An
Anthology of Short Novels*.) No author need apologize for
writing about death, a topic of such enormous interest that
it is rivaled only by sex. But if we think for a moment about

"The Death of Ivan Ilych," we realize that it is largely about the *life* of Ivan Ilych, or, more precisely, about his deathbed realization that he has scarcely lived. Despite the recurrent references to Ivan Ilych's illness, the story reveals not a morbid interest in illness and dying but a heartening interest in living.

The first sentence of the second part of the story makes this clear: "Ivan Ilych's life had been most simple and most ordinary and therefore most terrible." In the remainder of the story Tolstoy (clearly the narrator is Tolstoy, or someone so close to him that we need scarcely speak delicately of "the narrator") goes on to demonstrate the terribleness of this ordinariness. Superficially Ivan Ilych's life would seem to be unusual and successful: he climbs fairly high up the social ladder, achieves a substantial salary, has a wife, children, and an ample home, and he has some power which he savors even if he does not abuse it. But the point, of course, is that after he falls ill and nears death, he becomes aware -- as Tolstoy has kept the reader aware -- that Ivan Ilych's interests are so narrow, and even his vices so trivial, that however he may be envied he can scarcely be said to have lived. He learns this through sickness, which forces intense awareness of oneself, as anyone realizes who has had even so trivial a sickness as a running nose. And one of the facts about us, which we are scarcely aware of until we become sick, is that someday we will die.

Tolstoy makes it clear that, in a way, Ivan Ilych knew this: in a logic text he had learned that "Caius is a man, men are mortal, therefore Caius is mortal," but, Tolstoy says, these words "had always seemed to him correct as applied to Caius, but certainly not as applied to himself." And here we can digress for a moment on one of the differences between literature and philosophy. Literature, it has long been recognized, has a concreteness or immediacy that at least in some considerable degree forces the reader to sense or experience the reality that is being presented: to some degree we believe in and understand the experiences of the characters in good literature (at least in realistic prose fiction such as this story). *Why* do we identify with such figures? Probably for at least two reasons: (1) We are given a fairly convincing detailed picture of their surroundings, and (2) we are given revelations of character or psychological insights whose truth we recognize from our own experiences. Each of these two points may be discussed a bit.

Most novels, long or short, carefully build up a picture of the characters' surroundings. Thus, "The Death of Ivan Ilych" begins with a reference to an apparently public event ("the Melvinski trial") and to a public building ("the Law Courts"), specifies the name of a particular person, and moves through other people's names to the name of a newspaper. We know, of course, that we are reading fiction, but it is fiction that insists on facts, rather than fiction that begins "Once upon a time in a far-off country there lived a woodsman who had three sons." But it is not merely the specification of names of buildings, people, and newspapers that gives us a sense of a believable world. Tolstoy continually gives us a sense of the solidity of things. For example, describing the players beginning a card game Tolstoy mentions that "they dealt, bending the new cards to soften them." We need not look here for symbolism, we need not fancy that the cards, like Ivan Ilych, are being forced into a new shape; we can be content simply with our sense of the reality of this (fictional) card game. It is through such details, which pervade the story, that the writer gains our confidence. Illustrations need not be multiplied, but we might look briefly at one other scene before proceeding to the second point, the author's psychological astuteness. In the first section of the story there is a highly comic scene when Peter Ivanovich sits "on a low pouffe, the springs of which yielded spasmodically under his weight." There again, most literally, is the sense of the weight of things. When Peter must get up to assist the widow in detaching a shawl which catches on the carved edge of a table (again, convincing even if apparently irrelevant detail) "the springs of the pouffe, relieved of his weight, rose also and gave him a push." It probably is not fanciful to see here, in the pouffe's mechanical behavior, satiric commentary on the mechanical (conventional, unspontaneous) behavior of Peter and the widow, but it would be wrong to neglect the fact that Tolstoy also sees the pouffe as a pouffe, a thing with a density of its own, and it is through a world of believable things that his characters move.

Now for the second point, the revelation of convincing characters. Possibly the presentation of convincing *things* is a sort of sleight of hand whereby an author wins our confidence in his perceptions. After all, it does not follow that because a writer is perceptive enough to notice that card players bend new cards and that pouffes have springs, he is a shrewd perceiver of human nature. But in page after page Tolstoy does indeed give us shrewd perceptions of human nature. He catches the irritability and the hypersensitivity of a sick man, for example, in the scene when his partner "pushed the cards courteously and indulgently towards Ivan Ilych that he might have the pleasure of gathering them up without the trouble of stretching out his hand for them" and Ivan Ilych's mental response is "Does he think I am too weak to stretch out my arm?"

As we begin to read the story, perceiving the mutual insincerity which passes between Peter Ivanovich and the widow he is supposed to be consoling, and perceiving Ivan Ilych's shallowness, we may feel superior to the characters, but it soon becomes evident that although these people are not very amiable, we can scarcely look down on them. Too much is revealed about them that we recognize in ourselves. We have been pushed by pouffes, we have experienced "the complacent feeling that, 'it is he who is dead and not I,'" we have said to widows what we believe we are supposed to say, and -- most telling-- we know from experience the truth of Tolstoy's assertion that after Peter pressed the widow's hand because it was "the right thing," "both he and she were touched." That hurts, this perception that we are moved by our own calculating gestures.

Most of all, of course, we are concerned with Ivan Ilych, not with his widow or his acquaintances, and here again, we are compelled to recognize that we cannot take a superior attitude. We simply find him too recognizable, too human, too much ourself, to take refuge in thoughts of our superiority. Interestingly, he is *not* given much external characterization: he has a name, he is somewhat bald, he has a prominent nose and a graying beard, but he is not described in such detail as to become a "character" and therefore someone apart from us. The story, after all, is the story of Everyman: near the end of one's life one finds that death terrifies, and that one has not loved and therefore in any significant sense one has scarcely lived. Ivan Ilych very late and very painfully comes to an awareness of these things; his body racks him first into an awareness of physical existence and then into an awareness of spirit whereby he is at last able to recognize his lifetime of failure and to experience -- terribly late -- a compassion that banishes the fear of death. In a very crude sense, then, the story has a happy ending: a man in his last couple of hours experiences a pity for others that is perhaps indistinguishable from love and dies without fear; but Tolstoy does not let us off that easily with a comforting message. We continue to remember the agony of Ivan Ilych's dying months, and the waste of his life.

<u>Charlotte Perkins Gilman, "The Yellow Wallpaper."</u> The wife apparently is suffering from postpartum depression, and her physician-husband prescribes as a cure the things that apparently have caused her depression: isolation and inactivity. In this he acts in accord with Victorian medical theory that held that women -- more emotional, more nervous, more fanciful than men -- needed special protection if they were to combat

lunacy. As Gilman tells us in her autobiography, *The Living of Charlotte Perkins Gilman* (1935), the story (published in 1892) is rooted in the author's experience: after the birth of her child, Gilman became depressed and consulted Dr. S. Weir Mitchell (physician and novelist, named in the story), who prescribed a rest-cure: "Live as domestic a life as possible. Have your child with you all the time. Lie down an hour after each meal. Have but two hours intellectual life a day. And never touch pen, brush or pencil as long as you live." Gilman in fact tried this routine for a month, then took a trip to California, where she began writing, and recovered nicely. Thinking about Mitchell's plan later, Gilman concluded that such a way of life would have driven her crazy.

Although the prescribed treatment in the story is not exactly Mitchell's, it does seem clear enough that the smug husband's well-intended treatment is responsible for the wife's hallucinations of a woman struggling behind the wallpaper. The narrator is mad (to this degree the story resembles some of Poe's) but she is remarkably sane compared to her well-meaning husband and the others whose care for her is destructive. Elaine R. Hedges, in the afterword to the edition of *The Yellow Wallpaper* published by the Feminist Press (1973) comments on the narrator:

> At the end of the story the narrator both does and does not identify with the creeping women who surround her in her hallucinations. The women creep through the arbors and lanes and along the roads outside the house. Women must creep. The narrator knows this. She has fought as best she could against creeping. In her perceptivity and in her resistance lie her heroism (or heroineism). But at the end of the story, on her last day in the house, as she peels off yards and yards of wallpaper and creeps around the floor, she has been defeated. She is totally mad. But in her mad-sane way she has seen the situation of women for what it is [p. 53].

For a valuable survey of Gilman's life and work, see Millicent Bell's essay in *The New York Review of Books*, April 17, 1980.

Suggested Topics for Writing:

1. Characterize John as he probably sees himself, and then characterize him as the narrator sees him.
2. In the next-to-last paragraph the narrator says, "I've got out at last." What does she mean, and in what way does it make sense?
3. Trace the development of the narrator's mind, and with it trace the development of our attitude toward her.

James Joyce, "Araby." Probably the best discussion is in Cleanth Brooks and Robert Penn Warren, *Understanding Fiction*. The narrator of the story, presumably a mature man (cf. "her name was like a summons to all my foolish blood"), recounts a story of disillusionment. The first two paragraphs clearly establish the complacent middle-class world into which he is born -- the houses "conscious of decent lives within them" gaze with "imperturbable faces." This idea of decency is made concrete by the comment in the second paragraph that the priest's charity is evident in his will: he left all of his money to institutions and his furniture to his sister. (Probably even the sister was so decent that she too thought this was the right thing to do.) As a boy he had lived in a sterile atmosphere, a sort of fallen world (the house is in a "blind" or deadend street; the priest has died; a bicycle pump, once a device to inflate, is now rusty and unused; an apple tree is in the center of the garden in this fallen world; nearby are the odors of stable and garbage dumps), but he is quickened by various things, especially by Mangan's sister (unnamed to suggest that his love is almost spiritual?). He promises to visit "Araby" (a bazaar) and return with a gift for her. The boy for a while moves through a romantic religious world: he sees her "image," he imagines that he carries a "chalice," he hears the "litanies" and "chanting" of vendors, and he utters "strange prayers." Delayed by his uncle, whose inebriation is indicated by the uncle's "talking to himself," and by "the hall-stand rocking" (his parents seem not to be living; notice the emphasis on the boy's isolation throughout the story, e.g., his ride alone in the car of the train), he gets to the fair at closing time and he hears the clerks counting the day's receipts -- moneychangers in the temple. "The light was out. The upper part of the hall was now completely dark." The darkness and the preceding trivial conversations of a girl and two young men reveal (Joyce might have said epiphanize) the emptiness of the world. He has journeyed to a rich, exotic (religious?) world created by his imagination, and found it cold and trivial, as dead as the neighborhood he lives in. By the way, the boy's entry through the shilling entrance rather than through the sixpenny (children's) entrance signals his coming of age.

Suggested Topics for Writing:

1. Isolation in "Araby."
2. The function of religious imagery in "Araby."
3. The function of a journey in "Araby."

Franz Kafka, "The Metamorphosis." (The following discussion
is an abridgement of an afterword in our *Nine Modern Classics:
An Anthology of Short Novels*.) If we call something Shakespearean, the something is likely to be a passage of poetry;
if we call something Shavian, the something is likely to be a
play. But if we call something Kafkaesque, the something is
not likely to be literature, but an experience — a maddening
encounter with bureaucracy, or a supremely banal moment of
horror.

Horror fiction used to deal with misshapen people and strange
instruments of torture, but Kafka probably more than any other
literary figure changed all that, and gave us a literature of
commonplace horror: encounters with bewildering officials,
dreamlike efforts of ordinary people to clear up petty things,
incomprehensible interruptions in our routines, a sense of
isolation from one's fellows and even from oneself. These
experiences are set forth in a matter-of-fact style that
serves, by its passionless recording of precise details, to
relate them convincingly to the reader's daily life. "The
Metamorphosis" is somewhat unusual in its fantastic premise,
but even this story about a man who has turned into an insect
is told with no sense of wonder.

The sense of exile is Kafka's recurrent theme, and no writer
on Kafka fails to point out this deep sense of isolation; he
was a Jew in a Gentile world, a German speaker in Prague, a
victim of tuberculosis, neurotically estranged from his domi-
neering father, and a literary man in a bourgeois society. An
entry in his diary, where he imagines himself as some sort of
impotent winged creature, is of special interest to readers of
"The Metamorphosis," and it may help to reveal the sense of
isolation that he felt his literary gift has imposed on him:

> What will be my fate as a writer is very simple. My
> talent for portraying my dreamlike inner life has
> thrust all other matters into the background; my life
> has dwindled dreadfully, nor will it cease to dwindle.
> . . . I waver, continually fly to the summit of the
> mountain, but then fall back in a moment.

His "Letter to His Father," a lucid account of the sense of inferiority that his authoritarian father instilled in him, also
has some images that connect interestingly with "The Metamorphosis": Kafka's friends are, in his father's words, "vermin" and "fleas," and Kafka imagines his father replying to
the letter by calling Kafka a kind of "vermin" that "sucks
blood in order to sustain its own life." But what is especially important for us, since we are interested in Kafka's

novel rather than in his life, is a passage in which he describes a moment of intense humiliation and then -- astoundingly -- adds, "I was frantic with desperation and at such moments all my bad experiences in all spheres fitted magnificently together." "Magnificently" is the astounding word: the chaos and traumas sometimes cohered and he was able to make them into something magnificent.

Exactly what this magnificent thing in front of us, "The Metamorphosis," is, can be much debated, but debate tends to reduce it to simple formulas such as man's unconscious feeling of guilt, the Jew in a Gentile society, the writer in a bourgeois society, or the writer's inability to communicate his vision. Probably something of all of these interpretations, and a good many more, is in the novel; but, surely, as we read it, we respond, rather than interpret, and we respond at least partly because the emotions described in the story are recognizably our own. The first two or three pages, for instance, carefully record normal responses on awakening: "What about sleeping a little longer," "What an exhausting job I've picked," "A man needs his sleep," "Well, supposing he were to say he was sick." There are, of course, in addition to the astounding premise of a man who changes into a bug, strange dreamlike passages, such as those concerning the three lodgers, and Gregor's father's insistence on wearing his uniform even when off duty. But on the whole the story holds us not by its fantasy but by its realism, its patient recounting of familiar states of mind and its patient description of the insect.

These states of mind, doubtless occasionally felt in all ages, seem especially modern, and it is highly appropriate that Kafka chose for his hero, or antihero, a traveling salesman, for the salesman's profession necessarily imposes rootlessness and discontinuity upon him. One is tempted to say that Kafka depicts alienation -- the individual's sense that he is separated from his "real self" and forced to adopt a role that does not involve the "real self." But Gregor, at the start, is only intermittently aware that the life he leads is alien to his true self: he grumbles, of course, but he also takes pleasure in being the support of his family, and he is almost wholly devoted to his work. We are told that he does not go out of the house during the evenings but spends his time reading newspapers and railway timetables, and the only suggestions of a life other than his life of drudgery are his interest in fretwork and the pinup girl on the wall. Spineless, he is not so much a man who feels he is forced into the role of a bug, as he is a bug itself, which is why the story begins, rather than ends, with Gregor's metamorphosis. (But we cannot easily feel superior to Gregor; we somehow recognize that Kafka's image

of human feelings within an insect's body is a brilliant representation of our dual nature.) The remainder, and bulk, of
the story, recounts society's rejection of this drudge, and
his perception that he is utterly unloved, a perception that
causes him to cease to hang on to life. (This is Gregor's
most notable perception, but in the story there are a few
other passages indicating, curiously, that as a bug Gregor
occasionally is more perceptive than he has been earlier. The
description of his response to his sister's music is especially suggestive.) His family feels an enormous relief when
this bug dies, and Kafka takes some pains to let the reader
share in this relief, for the story -- even while it ends with
the parents plotting to marry off the daughter to some suitable husband -- concludes with references to "the open country"
(it began inside a bedroom, on a rainy and overcast day),
"vivacity," and the daughter rising and stretching. It is
almost as though the metamorphosis at the beginning is balanced
by another -- this one of the entire family. In his *Diaries*
Kafka refers cryptically to the "unreadable ending" of "The
Metamorphosis," but he did not suggest an alternative; he was
too honest to suggest that Gregor's death could be anything
other than a relief to Gregor and to all who knew him or heard
his story.

For a good discussion of "Metamorphosis" see Heinz Politzer,
Franz Kafka.

D. H. Lawrence, "The Horse Dealer's Daughter." Despite the
title the story is about Dr. Fergusson as well as about Mabel.
The deadness that characterizes her at the outset is later
seen to be relevant to him as well, though he has managed to
retain some vitality by keeping in touch with "the rough
strongly-feeling people." Mabel's lifelessness, consequent
upon the breakup of the family, brings her to her dead mother's
tomb (she feels secure in the churchyard); the landscape
("gray," "deadening," etc.) contributes to the bleakness. Her
devotion to her mother suggests not only a sort of spiritual
death but also a deep capacity for love, and it is therefore
fitting that her attempt to commit suicide by drowning herself
in the mucky winter pond turns out to lead to rebirth; the
doctor, though he cannot swim, enters the pond to rescue her,
goes over his head, and yet saves her. Both rise out of the
foul water changed persons, having undergone a sort of bap-
tism or rebirth from a womb. The change is also suggested by
the change of clothing, and in the references to fire and
light. Their new love is passionate and frightening, but that
is (presumably) a sign of its vitality. (Lawrence originally
called the story "The Miracle.") Kate Chopin's "The Story of

25

an Hour" (p. 23 in the text) somewhat similarly deals with a sort of rebirth, and can be usefully compared. There are discussions of Lawrence's story in Cleanth Brooks. J. T. Purser, and R. P. Warren, *An Approach to Literature*; Mark Schorer, *The Story*; Kingsley Widmer, *The Art of Perversity*; Sean O'Faolain, *Short Stories*; and T. H. McCabe, in *PMLA* 87 (1972), pp. 64-68.

Suggested Topics for Writing:

1. The uses of point of view in "The Horse Dealer's Daughter."
2. Setting as symbolic of life and death.

Katherine Anne Porter, "The Jilting of Granny Weatherall."

Students do not always understand that there are two narratives here: a narrative of a woman's dying hour and a narrative of the past that floods her mind. The old lady, a tough Southerner or Southwesterner with an intense love of life, has "weathered all," even a jilting; she had expected a groom, George, and was publicly disappointed when he failed to show up. Now, at her death, again a priest is in the house, and again she is disappointed or "jilted": the bridegroom (Christ) fails to appear. (It may be worthwhile to call attention to the parable of the wise and foolish virgins, in Matthew 25:1-13, where the bridegroom does appear, but the foolish virgins miss him.) The first jilting could in some measure be overcome, but the second is unendurable. Porter gives us the stream of Granny's consciousness, and if we are not always perfectly clear about details (did Hapsy die in childbirth?), we are nevertheless grateful for the revelation of an unfamiliar state of consciousness. By the way, the student may not realize why Hapsy (though dead) plays such an important role in Granny's consciousness. Hapsy, her last child, was "the one she had truly wanted." Presumably she had at last come to love her husband. On this point it is relevant to mention, too, that one of her sons is named George (presumably for the man who jilted her, and the other son is *not* named John, for his father, but Jimmy).

Suggested Topics for Writing:

1. The meaning of the title, "The Jilting of Granny Weatherall."
2. The reader's developing response to Ellen Weatherall.
3. Religious imagery in "The Jilting of Granny Weatherall."
4. The meaning of "duty" in "The Jilting of Granny Weatherall."
5. The two narratives of "The Jilting of Granny Weatherall."
6. The imagery of darkness and light in "The Jilting of Granny Weatherall."

Jean Rhys, "I Used to Live Here Once." The story is so short that one might almost think it must be a parable or fable, but surely it is not. There is no reason to squeeze a moral out of it, and indeed one can use this story along with a parable or fable to illustrate something of the range of storytelling: at one extreme, meaning or significance is primary, and at the other (as here), sheer happening with no "relevance" to us.

"I Used to Live Here Once" can be used to talk about foreshadowing, and since it is so short the entire story can be read aloud in class as a prelude to any discussion. Once we know how it ends (the woman discovers that she is dead), on rereading we see how cunningly contrived it is. The first thing that we encounter, the title, turns out not to be the mere casual statement that any of us might make when we visit a former residence; "I used to live here once" turns out to mean "I once was alive, I once inhabited the earth." And the first paragraph, describing a journey across a river, turns out also to be a journey across Styx, i.e., across the boundary between the world of the living and the world of the dead.

The second paragraph -- when we know how the story ends -- conveys a suggestion of the messiness of life here as it must appear to those in the next world. The third paragraph, calling attention to the unfamiliar "glassy" look of the sky, also suggests that something is not quite right, and then, at the end of the paragraph we get another reference to the "unfinished" or messy state of our daily world. The next paragraph plays the sense of familiarity against the sense of loss and strangeness.

The next three paragraphs, narrating her attempts to communicate with the children, end with her "longing to touch them," a natural action yet one that is chilling because although "her arms went out," we are not told that she did touch them. And indeed the atmosphere becomes literally chilling, for the boy, in the presence of this revenant, remarks, "Hasn't it gone cold all of a sudden," and we're told "Her arms fell to her sides" ("lifelessly," we almost add), whereas the living children are seen "running across the grass." In the final paragraph the protagonist and the reader alike come to see what really has -- from the title onward -- been going on.

James Thurber, "The Secret Life of Walter Mitty." Class discussion may begin with an examination of the point at which it is apparent that the story is comic. Anyone who knows Thurber's name will of course expect comedy, but not every student has heard of him. The first two sentences do not (on first reading reveal themselves as comic, though in hindsight one sees that at least the first sentence is from the world of inferior adventure stories. An alert reader may become suspicious of the third sentence with its "full-dress uniform" and its "heavily braided white cap pulled down rakishly over one cold gray eye." Suspicions are confirmed with "ta-pocketa-pocketa-pocketa-pocketa-pocketa-pocketa"; the ludicrous "eight-engine Navy hydraplane" and the cliché about the Old Man make the comedy unmistakable. Instructors may find it useful to introduce the concept of pathos, and to lead the class in a discussion of the relation of the pathetic to the tragic and to the comic. Here, of course, Mitty's daydreams are comic; we may pity him because of his weakness, but we can only laugh at his daydreams which (1) are so greatly in contrast with the actual events, and (2) are so indebted to bad movies and pulp magazines. For a brief discussion of pathos, and its relation to tragedy, see the discussion of Arthur Miller's *Death of a Salesman* in this manual. An interpretation of the story is in Brooks and Warren, *Understanding Fiction*; Charles S. Holmes, *The Clocks of Columbus*, is a useful study of Thurber. James Ellis, in *English Journal* 54 (1965), pp. 310-13, points out that Mitty's fantasies are made even more fantastic by various bits of misinformation. For example, Mitty the Sea Captain calls for "full strength in turret No. 3," mistakenly thinking that the turrets move the ship; the Surgeon nonsensically speaks of obstreosis (primarily a disease of cattle and pigs) of the ductal tract, and thinks coreopsis (a flower) is a disease; the Marksman refers to a 50.80 caliber pistol (its diameter would be more than four feet); the Pilot speaks of von Richtman but means von Richthofen.

Suggested Topics for Writing:

1. An analysis of the last scene in "Walter Mitty."
2. Pathos in "Walter Mitty."
3. The order of the fantasies in "Walter Mitty."

William Faulkner, "A Rose for Emily." The plot, of course, is Gothic fiction: a decaying mansion, a mysteriously silent servant, a corpse, necrophilia. And one doesn't want to discard the plot in a search for what it symbolizes; but it is also clear that the story is not only "about" Emily Grierson but also about the South's pride in its past (including its Emily-like effort to hold on to what is dead) and the guilt as well as the grandeur of that past. Inevitably much classroom discussion centers on Miss Emily's character, but a proper discussion of her character entails a discussion of the narrator. (In what follows we briefly summarize an essay on this topic by John Daremo, originally printed in S. Barnet, *A Short Guide to Writing about Literature*.) The unnamed narrator is never precisely identified. Sometimes he seems to be an Innocent Eye, a recorder of a story whose implications escape him. Sometimes he seems to be coarse: he mentions "old Lady Wyatt, the crazy woman," he talks easily of "niggers," and he confesses that because he and other townspeople felt that Miss Emily's family "held themselves a little too high for what they really were," the townspeople "were not pleased exactly, but vindicated" when at thirty she was still unmarried. But if his feelings are those of common humanity, he *knows* what these feelings are, and he thus helps us to know ourselves. We therefore pay him respectful attention, and we notice that on the whole he is compassionate (note especially his sympathetic understanding of her insistence for three days that her father is not dead). True, Miss Emily earns our respect by her aloofness and her strength of purpose (e.g., when she publicly appears in the buggy with Homer Barron, and when she cows the druggist and the alderman), but if we speak of her aloofness and her strength of purpose rather than of her arrogance and her madness, it is because the narrator's imaginative sympathy guides us. And the narrator is the key to the apparently curious title: presumably the telling of this tale itself is the rose, the community's tribute (for the narrator insistently speaks of himself as "we") to the intelligible humanity in a woman whose unhappy life might seem monstrous to less sympathetic observers.

William Faulkner, "Barn Burning." Against his vision of the ideals of the Confederacy, embodied in Major de Spain and Colonel Sartoris in much of Faulkner's writing, Faulkner sets his vision of a more widely held ideal -- cunning and self-centeredness, embodied in the Snopes family. (Flem Snopes, the older brother in "Barn Burning," is a major character in *The Town*, *The Mansion*, and *The Hamlet*; Abner Snopes, the father in "Barn Burning," is a lesser character in *The Unvanquished* and in *The Hamlet*. But the boy, Colonel Sartoris Snopes, does not appear in the novels.)

It would be wrong, however, to see the Snopes family -- and especially, here, Abner Snopes -- as merely contemptible. Abner's single-mindedness, however unlovely and destructive, gives him a hero's aspect, for example when he walks resolutely on toward the great house and refuses to deviate by even a single step that would enable him to avoid stepping in the horse-dung. Abner Snopes has, we might say, something of the air of the tragic hero who, like Job confronted with what seems to be an assault on his integrity, will maintain his own ways even before God. He has, in Faulkner's words, a "ferocious conviction in the rightness of his own actions." Or, to quote again, a deep sense of the importance of "the preservation of integrity, else breath were not worth the breathing." This second passage, by the way, comes in the discussion of "the niggard blaze" that is part of Snopes's way of life. Coupled with the burning barns, it suggests that Snopes is a Promethean figure -- not the Prometheus of the ancients, who gave fire to man out of pity, but a romantic Promethean figure who sets his blaze in defiance of authority.

As we read "Barn Burning" we are reminded of Alfred North Whitehead's comment that tragedy shows us "the remorseless working of things," an action that cannot be stopped, partly because the hero, insisting on asserting himself, is determined that it shall not be stopped. We can scarcely *like* Snopes, but we can scarcely fail to admire (especially in the older sense of "wonder at," "be awed by") him. Indeed, if we compare Major de Spain's justifiable but somewhat fussy anger over the rug ("You must realize you have ruined that rug") with Snopes's smoldering rage at any limitations imposed on him, we may feel that Snopes is by far the more vital figure. One notes, too, and cannot dismiss, Snopes's charge that Major de Spain's big white house has been built out of "sweat. Nigger sweat. Maybe it ain't white enough to suit him. Maybe he wants to mix some white sweat with it." We may feel that in large measure Snopes's ruthlessness proceeds from a sense of social inferiority, but we can scarcely deny that he offers a telling criticism of his social superiors.

Finally, a few words about Sarty, the boy. He too is a sort of hero, moved by the most painful kind of conflict -- not good with evil but good with good, for he must choose between his sense of decency and his sense of loyalty to the family.

Suggested Topics for Writing:

1. Point of view in "Barn Burning." (Sarty is not the narrator, but we hear the story as the boy perceives it. We enter his mind only; when the language used to present his thoughts is clearly not his own language, it is usually given in italics.)
2. Is Faulkner on Major de Spain's side, or Abner Snopes's, or both, or neither?
3. Is Sarty's action at the end adequately motivated?

Eudora Welty, "A Worn Path." In an essay in *The Georgia Review* (Winter 1979), Eudora Welty (talking chiefly of her first

story, "The Death of a Traveling Salesman") says that her
characters "rise most often from the present" but her plots
are indebted to "the myths and fairy tales I steeped myself in
as a young reader. . . . By the time I was writing stories I
drew on them as casually as I drew on the daily newspaper or
the remarks of my neighbors."

Clearly "A Worn Path" draws on the myth of the phoenix, the
golden bird that periodically consumes itself in flames so
that it may be renewed. Phoenix Jackson renews her ancient
body on each visit to the doctor's remote office. The chief
clues: the woman's name ("Phoenix"); the description of her
early in the story (her stick makes a sound "like the chirping
of a solitary little bird"; "a golden color ran underneath,
and the two knobs of her cheeks were illuminated by a yellow
burning under the dark"); a reference to cyclic time ("I bound
to go to town, mister. The time come around," and the time is
Christmas); her "ceremonial stiffness" in the doctor's office;
and, finally, the words "Phoenix rose carefully."

But the myth is wonderfully supported by details, details that
are strictly irrelevant (e.g., Phoenix's deception of the
hunter, which nets her a nickel, and her cadging of a nickel's
worth of pennies from the nurse), but that makes the character
thoroughly convincing.

The story, finally, is (as Eudora Welty has said in "Is Phoenix
Jackson's Grandson Really Dead?" in *The Eye of the Story*) about
"the deep-grained habit of love," or, we might say, about faith
that a mission of love is life-sustaining. "A Worn Path" can
be, Welty even says, an allegory of the life of a writer:
"Your only guide . . . is your sureness about what this subject is. Like Phoenix, you work all your life to find your
way, through all the obstructions and the false appearances
and the upsets you may have brought on yourself, to reach a
meaning. . . . And finally too, like Phoenix, you have to
assume that what you are working in aid of is life, not death."

Suggested Topic for Writing:

Is the story sentimental? (We would say "no," for several
reasons: Phoenix, though old and -- at moments -- mentally
failing, is dignified and never self-pitying; the writer,
letting Phoenix tell her own story, never asks us to pity
Phoenix; Phoenix exhibits both a sense of humor and a sense
of self-reliance, and on those occasions when she needs help
she exhibits no embarrassment.)

Ralph Ellison, "King of the Bingo Game." Inevitably, discussion will center on whether or not the story is true to the black experience and, second, whether or not it is meaningful to whites as a revelation of this experience. But perhaps one can go further and suggest that in some degree the story is about a man's attempt (not only a black man's, but any man's) to control his fate by holding on to the power that may come into his hands. Most of the time we feel helpless -- often even victimized -- in a world we never chose, but there may come a moment when, in the master of ceremonies' facetious term, we are "one of the chosen people," i.e., when destiny seems to be cooperating with our aspiration, and we hang on to such a moment as best we can, feeling that at last we are "running the show."

In an interview in *Writers at Work, Second Series*, Ellison discusses *Invisible Man* at length, but some of his comments are relevant to "King of the Bingo Game." Asked how a black writer can "escape provincialism when his literature is concerned with a minority," he replied: "All novels are about certain minorities: the individual is a minority. The universal in the novel -- and isn't that what we're all clamoring for these days? -- is reached only through the depiction of the specific man in a specific circumstance." Of black folklore he says, "One ironic witness to the beauty and the universality of this art is the fact that the descendants of the very men who enslaved us can now sing the spirituals and find in the singing an exaltation of their own humanity."

Shirley Jackson, "The Lottery." The story is of course based on fertility rituals of the sort described in Sir James Frazer's *The Golden Bough*: a community is purged of its evil, and fertility is ensured, by the sacrifice of an individual, i.e., a scapegoat. "Lottery in June, corn be heavy soon," Mr. Warner says. In "The Lottery" the method of execution is stoning, which Frazer reports was a method used in ancient Athens.

Until the last six paragraphs we think we are reading a realistic story about decent small-town life. Probably on rereading we notice that, despite all the realism, the time and the place are never specified; we may feel we are reading about a twentieth-century New England town, but we cannot document this feeling. On rereading, too, we pay more attention to the early references to stones, and to the general nervousness, and of course we see the importance of Tessie Hutchinson's outburst. (Consult Helen E. Nebeker, "'The Lottery': Symbolic Tour de Force," *American Literature* 46 (1974), 100-07.) With the last six paragraphs the horror comes, and it is described in the same matter-of-fact objective tone used in the earlier part of the story. Inevitably a discussion turns to the question, Does the story have any meaning for a modern society? Students in the 1980s may have to be reminded that a lottery was used as recently as the Vietnam War to pick the people who would be subject to slaughter. In *Come Along with Me* Shirley Jackson discusses the furor "The Lottery" evoked after its original publication in *The New Yorker* in 1948. Lenemaja Friedman, in *Shirley Jackson*, reports that Jackson said of the theme: "Explaining just what I hoped the story to say is very difficult. I suppose, I hoped, by setting a particularly brutal ancient rite in the present and in my own village, to shock the story's readers with a graphic demonstration of the pointless violence and general inhumanity in their own lives." On the other hand, we are not at all sure that anyone -- even the author of this story -- should press it for its meaning or theme. Formulations such as "Society engages in ritualized slaughter," or "Society disguises its cruelty, even from itself," or "Even decent people seek scapegoats" do not quite seem to fit. Isn't it possible that the story is an effective shocker, signifying nothing? We notice, too, the significance of the date -- June 27 is close to the summer solstice, the season for planting -- and we notice the significance of some of the names: the ritual is presided over by Mr. Summers, the first man to draw a lot is Mr. Adams, and conservative warnings are uttered by Mr. Warner.

Suggested Topics for Writing:

1. Foreshadowing in "The Lottery."
2. Is "The Lottery" more than a shocker?

Flannery O'Connor, "A Good Man Is Hard to Find." In the early part of this story the grandmother is quite as hateful as the rest of the family -- though students are not likely to understand at first that her vapid comments and her moral clichés and her desire to be thought "a lady" are offensive in their own way. Her comment, "People are certainly not nice like they used to be," can perhaps be used to convince students of her mindlessness and even of her lack of charity.

The Misfit, like Jesus, was "buried alive"; he believes that "Jesus thown everything off balance," and he finds no satisfaction in life (i.e., his life without grace). Life is either a meaningless thing in which all pleasure is lawful (and, ironically, all pleasure turns to ashes) or it derives its only meaning from following Jesus. The Misfit, though he does not follow Jesus, at least sees that the materialistic view of life is deficient. Confronted by the suffering of the Misfit, the nagging and shallow grandmother suddenly achieves a breakthrough, and is moved by love. She had earlier recognized The Misfit ("'You're The Misfit!' she said. 'I recognized you at once.'") and now she has a further recognition of him as "one of her own children," i.e., as a suffering fellowman. Faced with death, she suddenly becomes aware of her responsibility: "the grandmother's head cleared for an instant," and she says "You're one of my own children." This statement is not merely an attempt to dissuade the Misfit from from killing her; contrast it with her earlier attempts, when, for example, she says, "I know you come from nice people! Pray! Jesus, you ought not to shoot a lady. I'll give you all the money I've got." Rather, at last her head is "cleared." This moment of grace transfigures her and causes her death. The Misfit is right when he says, "She would of been a good woman if it had been somebody there to shoot her every minute of her life." On the "moment of grace" in O'Connor's fiction see *College English* 27 (December 1965), pp. 235-39, and R. M. Vande Kiefte in *Sewanee Review* 76 (1968), pp. 337-56. Vande Kiefte notes that the description of the dead grandmother ("her legs crossed under her like a child's and her face smiling up at the cloudless sky") suggests that death has jolted the grandmother out of her mere secular decency into the truth of eternal reality. See also Martha Stephens, *The Question of Flannery O'Connor*. Flannery O'Connor herself has commented usefully on this story in *Mystery and Manners*, pp. 107-14. She suggests that The Misfit is "a prophet gone wrong," and that "the real heart of the story" is when the grandmother "realizes, even in her limited way, that she is responsible for the man before her and joined to him by ties of kinship which have their roots deep in the mystery she has merely been prattling about so far."

Suggested Topics for Writing:

1. The Misfit and Christ.
2. The use of foreshadowing.
3. The grandmother's perception.

Flannery O'Connor, "Revelation." This story, like Miss O'Connor's "A Good Man Is Hard to Find," is concerned with a moment of grace, which most obviously begins when Mary Grace hurls a book at Mrs. Turpin -- an action somewhat parallel to The Misfit's assault on the grandmother. The doctor's office contains a collection of wretched human beings whose physical illness mirrors their spiritual condition. There is abundant comedy ("The nurse ran in, then out, then in again"), but these people are treated sympathetically too. Mrs. Turpin's pitiful snobbery -- especially her desperate effort to rank people in the eyes of God -- is comic and horrible but it at least reveals an uneasiness beneath her complacency, an uneasiness that finally compares well with the monumental hatred that characterizes Mary Grace. Yet Mary Grace, a pimply girl, *is* a messenger of grace. And so when the blow comes (from a book nicely called *Human Development*), it is not in vain. The girl's accusation ("Go back to hell where you came from, you old wart hog") strikes home, and later, among the pigs which Mrs. Turpin so solicitously cleans, the message produces a revelation, a revelation that forces upon her an awareness of the inadequacy of "virtue" (her horrible concept of respectability) as she has known it. Man's virtue is of as little value to fallen men as a hosing-down is to a pig; in her vision she sees that even virtue or respectability is burned away in the movement toward heaven. On the one hand, some students have difficulty seeing that Mrs. Turpin is not simply a stuffy hypocrite; on the other, some students have difficulty seeing that her respectability is woefully inadequate and must be replaced by a deeper sympathy. But perhaps students have the greatest difficulty in reconciling the comic aspects of the story with its spiritual depth, and here the instructor can probably not do much more than read some passages and hope for the best. Consult Sister Kathleen Feeley, *Flannery O'Connor*; do not consult Stanley Edgar Hymen, *Flannery O'Connor*.

John Updike, "A & P." It may be useful for students to characterize the narrator and to see if occasionally Updike slips. Isn't "crescent," in the third sentence, too apt a word for a speaker who a moment later says, "She gives me a little snort" and "If she'd been born at the right time they would have burned her over in Salem"? If this is a slip, it is more than compensated for by the numerous expressions that are just right. Like "Guests of the Nation," "A & P" is a first-person story, and in its way it, too, is about growing up. Students should try to characterize the narrator as precisely as possible. Notice his hope that the girls will observe his heroic pose, and notice, too, his admission that he doesn't want to hurt his parents. His belief (echoing Lengel's) that he will "feel this for the rest of his life" is also adolescent. But his assertion for the girls' innocence is attractive and brave.

Suggested Topics for Writing:

1. Sheep and Goats in "A & P."
2. Sammy: Comic yet Heroic? (Consult P. A. Gilbert, in *English Journal* 54 [1965], 577-84.)

<u>Donald Barthelme, "The School."</u> The narrator is a not-too-
bright but well-meaning teacher (caring for trees will give
the children a sense of responsibility) who rather desperately
tries to see the educational advantages of calamity. Thus,
in the third paragraph, the speaker notes that the children
"at least now . . . know not to overwater" herbs, and "not to
carry [white mice] around in plastic bags." Edgar tries to do
the job according to the book ("the lesson plan called for a
tropical-fish input at that point"), but life -- or, rather,
death -- keeps breaking in. (By the way, in class one might
discuss the reasons why Barthelme may have called the teacher
Edgar instead of, say, Kent or Scott.) Although at first
glance the story may seem to consist of meandering memories,
it has a sure structure: it begins with the death of some
lower forms of life (trees, herbs, snakes, fish, mice, and
gerbils), moves to a puppy, then (in the middle) to several
children, parents, and grandparents. And then, just after the
middle, with the theme of death out in the open, things go
screwy; the children talk in the clichés of a teacher ("and
they said, is death that which gives meaning to life?" "Isn't
death . . . a fundamental datum?"), and the teacher gets yet
more simpleminded: "I said, yes, maybe." Near the end, in
response to the students' demand for "an assertion of value,"
Edgar begins to demonstrate love by embracing and kissing
Helen, and at the very end the world of the classroom becomes
utterly surreal when a gerbil knocks on the door and enters.
The story ends here, but presumably the gerbil will meet the
fate of his predecessors, and thus the reader and the author
together round off the narrative.

<u>Joyce Carol Oates, "Where Are You Going, Where Have You Been?"</u>
Oates has said that she wrote the story after reading about a
killer in the Southwest and after hearing Bob Dylan's song,
"It's All Over Now, Baby Blue." One line of Dylan's song
("The vagabond who's standing at your door"), is clearly related to the story, and note that in the story itself Connie
wishes "it were all over." The story has affinities with "The
Demon Lover," printed in Chapter 8: the demon lover has "music
on every hand," and Connie "was hearing music in her head,"
and later Arnold and Ellie, in the car, listen to the same
radio station that Connie, in the house, listens to; the demon
lover's ship has "masts o the beaten gold," and Arnold's car
is "painted gold." The first sentence tells us that Connie
"Had a quick nervous giggling habit of craning her neck to
glance into mirrors." Her mother attributes it to vanity, and
indeed Connie does think she is pretty, but a more important
cause is insecurity. Connie's fear that she has no identity
sometimes issues in her wish that "she herself were dead and

it were all over with." "Everything about her had two sides,"
which again suggests an incoherent personality. Arnold Friend
has a hawklike nose, thick black lashes, an ability to see what
is going on in remote places, a curious (lame) foot, a taste
for strange bargains, incantatory speech, an enchanted subordinate, and a charismatic personality, and all in all he is a
sort of diabolic figure who can possess Connie, partly because
he shows her an enormous concern that no one else has shown
her. (The possession ["I'll come inside you, where it's all
secret"] is possession of her mind as well as of her body.)
Having said this, we should add that Oates says in an interview in *Commonweal* (5 December 1969), that although she at
first thought her fiction was indebted to Flannery O'Connor,
she has come to see that in O'Connor there is always a religious dimension whereas in her own fiction "there is only the
natural world."

Suggested Topics for Writing:

1. The sense of evil in "Where Are You Going?"
2. Alienation in "Where Are You Going?"

Toni Cade Bambara, "The Lesson." It would be hard to find a
less strident and more delightful story preaching revolution.
At its heart "The Lesson" calls attention to the enormous ine-
equity in the distribution of wealth in America, and it suggests that black people ought to start thinking about "what
kind of society it is in which some people can spend on a toy
what it would cost to feed a family of six or seven" for a
year. That the young narrator does not quite get the point of
Miss Moore's lesson -- and indeed steals Miss Moore's money --
is no sign that the lesson has failed. (Presumably Miss Moore
doesn't much care about the loss of her money; the money is
well lost if it helps the narrator, who plans to spend it, to
see the power of money.) In any case, Sugar gets the point,
and the narrator has been made sufficiently uneasy ("I sure
want to punch somebody in the mouth") so that we sense she
will later get the point: "I'm goin . . . to think this day
through." The last line of the story seems to refer to her
race to a bakery, but it has larger implications: "Ain't no-
body gonna beat me at nuthin."

Suggested Topic for Writing:

See Question 2 under Alice Walker's "Everyday Use," immediately
following.

<u>Alice Walker</u>, "<u>Everyday Use</u>." The title, like most other titles, is significant, though the significance appears only gradually. This significance, of course, is not limited to the fact that Dee believes that Maggie will use the quilts for "everyday use"; on reflection we see the love, in daily use, between the narrator and Maggie, and we contrast it with Dee's visit -- a special occurrence -- as well as with Dee's idea that the quilts should not be put to everyday use. The real black achievement, then, is not the creation of works of art that are kept apart from daily life; rather, it is the everyday craftsmanship and the everyday love shared by people who cherish and sustain each other. That Dee stands apart from this achievement is clear (at least on rereading) from the first paragraph, and her pretensions are suggested as early as the fourth paragraph, where we are told that she thinks "orchids are tacky flowers." Her lack of any real connection with her heritage is made explicit (even before the nonsense about using the churn top as a centerpiece) as early as the paragraph in which she asks if Uncle Buddy whittled the dasher, and Maggie quietly says that Henry whittled it. Still, Dee is confident that she can "think of something artistic to do with the dasher." Soon we learn that she sees the quilts not as objects of use but only as decorative works; Maggie, however, will use the quilts, and she even knows how to make them. Dee talks about the black "heritage" but Maggie and the narrator embody the heritage, and they experience a degree of contentment that eludes Dee.

Suggested Topics for Writing:

1. "Everyday Use" is by a black writer. If it were by a white writer, would it be offensive to blacks? Is it offensive to blacks *anyway*?

2. Compare "Everyday Use" with Bambara's "The Lesson" (p. 351). Consider the following suggestions: Characterize the narrator of each story and compare them. Compare the settings and how they function in each story. What is Miss Moore trying to teach the children in "The Lesson"? Why does Sylvia resist learning it? In "Everyday Use" what does Dee try to teach her mother and sister? Why do they resist her lesson? How are objects (such as quilts, toys) used in each story? How in each story does the first person narration enlist and direct our sympathies?

7

OBSERVATIONS ON THE NOVEL

It sometimes seems that books about the novel (or books including some discussion of the novel) are as numerous as novels. Among the commentaries of the last few decades that we have found valuable are:

> Robert Martin Adams, *Strains of Discord*
> Robert Alter, *Partial Magic: The Novel as a Self-Conscious Genre*
> Miriam Allott, *Novelists on the Novel*
> Wayne C. Booth, *The Rhetoric of Fiction*
> William H. Gass, *Fiction and the Figures of Life*
> Barbara Hardy, *The Appropriate Form*
> W. J. Harvey, *Character and the Novel*
> Robert Liddell, *Robert Liddell on the Novel*
> (a combined edition of *A Treatise on the Novel* and *Some Principles of Fiction*)
> David Lodge, *The Language of Fiction*
> Mary McCarthy, *On the Contrary*
> Robert Scholes and Robert Kellogg, *The Nature of Narrative*
> Philip Stevick, ed., *The Theory of the Novel*

But this is mere stalling. The question is, What novel to teach? The only time we experience any success in teaching a novel in an introductory course is when the novel is fairly short. Which means that we have failed miserably with *Portrait of a Lady*, *Bleak House*, and *The Brothers Karamazov* -- and even with *Crime and Punishment*. Our moderate successes are limited to traditional favorites of freshman English, things like

> *The Great Gatsby*
> *Hard Times*
> *Heart of Darkness*
> *Miss Lonelyhearts*
> *Notes from the Underground*
> *A Portrait of the Artist as a Young Man*
> *The Stranger*

Among more recent titles that work well are:

Chinua Achebe, *Things Fall Apart*
Anthony Burgess, *A Clockwork Orange*
Evan S. Connell, Jr., *Mrs. Bridge*
Graham Greene, *The Human Factor*
Brian Moore, *The Lonely Passion of Judith Hearne*
Sylvia Plath, *The Bell Jar*
Philip Roth, *The Ghost Writer*
Anne Tyler, *A Slipping Down Life*

Experienced teachers do not need us to suggest these titles; inexperienced teachers will perhaps do best if they choose a short novel that they read and enjoyed when they were freshmen or sophomores.

8

NARRATIVE POETRY

We print two literary ballads in Chapter 16, "A Collection of Poems" -- Keats's "La Belle Dame sans Merci" and Hardy's "Ah, Are You Digging on My Grave." Albert B. Friedman, in *The Viking Book of Folk Ballads*, reissued as *The Penguin Book of Folk Ballads*, gives additional versions of "Sir Patrick Spence," a comic version of "The Three Ravens," an American undemonic version of "The Demon Lover" (called "James Harris"), and an American version of "Edward." An American version of "Edward" is recorded on an album, *Child Ballads Traditional in the United States*, 1, issued by the Library of Congress (AAFS L57). Some of these may be useful in class discussion.

"The Three Ravens," like many other ballads, is filled with mystery: How did the knight die? Why does the doe bury him? Is the doe his lover? But against these uncertainties the poem gives us considerable detail: there are two ravens, the field is "green" (death and life coexist), hounds and hawks loyally guard the knight, and the doe cares for his corpse, protecting it from the birds who would make it their "breakfast." Having given us five stanzas in which death and life, and bodily self-satisfaction and loyalty are juxtaposed, the poem goes on in its next four stanzas to show us only gentleness and self-sacrifice. The final stanza, with its reference to a "leman," pretty clearly indicates that the pregnant doe is the knight's beloved, and, equally important, suggests that even though the knight is dead, his life was a sort of triumph since it earned such loyalty. The last stanza offers explicit moralizing, but the poem as a whole has *shown*, not preached.

"The Twa Corbies," of course, unlike "The Three Ravens," is a poem about *dis*loyalty -- of hound, hawk, and lady -- but we should not overlook the cozy, though macabre, domesticity of the fourth stanza, in which the corbies plan to dine and to patch their nest.

Bertrand Bronson, in *The Ballad as Song*, suggests that "Edward" may not be a pure folk ballad. Perhaps the strongest evidence of a "literary" touch is the fact that the surprise ending in

the last line -- which forces us to reconstruct our understanding of the mother -- is unusual for a ballad. In traditional ballads, Bronson points out, people ask questions in
order to learn what they do not know (or, in the case of
riddling ballads, in order to test someone), but in "Edward"
the questions and answers serve a sophisticated technique of
character revelation and of plot-telling. By the way, the
motifs of questions and answers and last will and testament,
found in "Edward," are also in "Lord Randal," which is fairly
well known among undergraduates.

Discussion of the questions that follow "Sir Patrick Spence"
ought to fill a good part of the hour and ought to help students to see the virtues in this great ballad. One might also
call attention to the fact that the poem begins not with Sir
Patrick -- whose initial appearance is effectively held off
and built up to -- and to the fact that the first lines, with
their reference to the king drinking, suggest a life of courtly
ease that contrasts with Sir Patrick's life of seamanship.
But notice too the dark or tragic implication in the second
line: the wine is "blude-reid." And we should also call attention to the contrast between the nobles, who are "loath" to
wet their shoes, and Sir Patrick, who is not eager for the
trip and is much more than "loath," for he knows that the trip
is virtually a death-mission. The nobles are associated with
ladies with fans and combs. The courtiers will be mourned by
the ladies, but we are not told of any mourners for Sir Patrick.
However, we see Sir Patrick as master of the lords in death by
virtue of having done his duty with full awareness.

Suggested Topic for Writing:

Understatement in "Sir Patrick Spence" (or, a slightly different way of putting it: Things unsaid in "Sir Patrick
Spence"). Though some instructors find it useful to assign
literary ballads (e.g., Keats's "La Belle Dame sans Merci")
when teaching popular ballads, we prefer to assign "La Belle
Dame" when discussing symbolism. For a discussion of "Sir
Patrick Spence," see Brooks and Warren, *Understanding Poetry*,
4th ed., pp. 25-26.

There is a wealth of information about the origin of "John
Henry" in Guy B. Johnson, *John Henry*, and in Louis W. Chappell,
John Henry. These books, and many other scholarly writings on
John Henry, are summarized in Richard M. Dorson, "The Career
of 'John Henry,'" *Western Folklore* 24 (1965), pp. 155-63, reprinted in *Mother Wit from the Laughing Barrel*, Alan Dundes,
ed. Albert B. Friedman, *The Penguin Book of Folk Ballads*,
prints six versions, and the song has often been recorded,

e.g., by Huddie Leadbetter, *Leadbelly's Last Sessions*, Vol. I, Part Two (Folkways Records FA 2941 C/D). Although "John Henry" was composed by blacks, sung by blacks, sung to blacks, and is about a black hero, Eldridge Cleaver suggests (*Soul on Ice*, p. 164) that it suits the purposes of white racism: the black is all Body and no Brain. There is something to this view; though ballads are scarcely likely to celebrate intellectual activity, when one thinks about the matter one notices that ballads celebrating a white folk hero normally give him a touch of cunning and make him a fighter against injustice (e.g., Jesse James "had a hand and a heart and a brain," and he "stole from the rich, and he gave to the poor"). "John Henry" celebrates only physical strength (and sometimes sexual strength, in the reference to his women). But the vast majority of ballads celebrating white heroes are rather unimpressive sentimental pieces; "John Henry," however limited its view, has an aesthetic excellence that endures. And after all, no one expects any work of art to tell the *whole* truth.

Kennedy's "In a Prominent Bar" begins, as a fair number of ballads do, by establishing a scene, and then introduces a speaker. (Cf., "The Twa Corbies.") The speaker moralizes her story; the moral is *carpe diem*, a motif discussed in Chapter 10 in connection with Herrick's "To the Virgins." (If the instructor wishes to get into the matter of persona now, the two poems can be effectively compared.) Very few traditional ballads include such moralizing -- "The Three Ravens" is thus unusual -- but broadside ballads often enough do encourage the hearer to learn a lesson, though the lesson is less likely to be "seize the day" than to be a sober bourgeois admonition to keep to the path of righteousness.

"Eleanor Rigby" is not, of course, a traditional ballad, but it can be effectively studied in a context of ballads and as a bridge to lyric poetry. The Beatles' version of the song is in their album *Revolver* (Capitol Records ST 2576).

43

9

LYRIC POETRY

One can engage in more profitable activities than in fretting about whether a given poem is a narrative poem or a lyric, but the topic is worth at least a little thought. Something, of course, depends on the way in which the text is rendered. Spirituals, for instance, often have considerable narrative content, and yet one feels that their affinities are with the lyric -- that the story is subordinate to the state of mind. This sense of lyrical meditation is, of course, heightened by the refrains -- repetitions that do not advance the story and that help to communicate and to induce a visionary state. An instructor who wants to pursue this topic may want to discuss such works as "Didn't My Lord Deliver Daniel," "Go Down, Moses," and "Joshua Fit the Battle of Jericho."

There is much fascinating material about the theory of nineteenth-century lyric poetry in M. H. Abrams, *The Mirror and the Lamp*. See also C. Day Lewis, *The Lyric Impulse*.

Versions of "Michael" were in print in the 1870s, and the song is still popular. Among effective recordings is one by Pete Seeger on Columbia (CS 9717). "Careless Love" easily leads to a discussion of the blues. Here is a brief part of Ralph Ellison's comment on the genre in an essay on Richard Wright in Ellison's *Shadow and Act:* "Their attraction lies in this, that they at once express both the agony of life and the possibility of conquering it through sheer toughness of spirit. They fall short of tragedy only in that they provide no solution, offer no scapegoat but the self."

"Western Wind" has been much discussed; a brief summary of the main essays is in *Explicator* 15 (February 1957), Item 28. If the instructor's taste runs to black humor he may wish to quote P. Dehn's "O nuclear wind, when wilt thou blow / That the small rain down can rain? / Christ, that my love were in my arms, / And I had my arms again."

A reader tends, of course, to think of Emily Dickinson as the speaker of "Wild Nights," and therefore is perhaps shocked by the last stanza, in which a woman apparently takes on the phallic role of a ship mooring in a harbor. But perhaps the poem is spoken by a man. (In one of her poems the speaker refers to "my brown cigar," and in "A narrow Fellow in the Grass" -- included in our book -- the speaker identifies himself as male in lines 11-12.) In any case (to touch on material in our first question in the text) the sexuality of the lovers can be unrestrained ("Done with the Compass -- / Done with the Chart!") because they are "Rowing in Eden," i.e., in a paradise governed by its own law, safe (at least for "Tonight") from the surrounding storm.

We don't find the poem sentimental, chiefly because it is brief, controlled, and (in "To-night") it does not claim too much.

In *Explicator* 25 (January 1967), Item 44, James T. Connelly pointed out that in letter No. 332 (T. H. Johnson's edition, *Letters*, vol. II, p. 463) Dickinson writes, "Dying is a wild Night and a new road." Looking at the poem in the light of this letter, Connelly concludes that "to die is to experience a wild night on a turbulent, surging sea. Only by plunging into this uncharted sea of Death can one at last reach the port of rest and calm. The poem, thus considered, is an apparent death wish: a personification and apostrophe to Death whose presence and company are paradoxically exhilerating luxury." We are unconvinced, partly because the poem speaks not of "a wild Night" but of "Wild Nights," and we cannot see how the plural form lends itself to his reading.

Though perhaps when we first think of blues we think of songs of disappointed love, blues include songs concerned with other kinds of loneliness, and some at least implicitly relate this loneliness to an oppressive society that is built on segregation and that engenders wandering and alienation. Hughes's "Evenin' Air Blues," then, is genuinely related to the blues tradition, though not surprisingly the note of social protest is a little more evident. The last stanza, chiefly by virtue of its first line, seems to make a natural conclusion, but as in most blues, the stanzas can pretty much stand independently; perhaps less blues-like is the perfection of the rhyme (one almost feels that the single near-rhyme [by the standards of standard English], *fine:mind*, in the first stanza, is a conscious imitation of such blues rhymes as *ride:by* or *dime:mine*). The blues often uses a three-line stanza in which the second line repeats the first; Hughes's six-line stanza, in which the fourth line repeats the second, is a variation on the usual form.

Whitman's "A Noiseless Patient Spider" is in free verse, a form discussed later in the text in connection with Whitman's "When I Heard the Learn'd Astronomer," but most instructors find it appropriate to say a few words about the form at this stage. In fact, of course, the poem is not terribly "free"; each stanza has five lines, helping to establish the similitude of spider and soul, and the first line of each stanza is relatively short, the other lines being longer to help establish the idea of "venturing, throwing." The near-rhyme at the end helps to tie up the poem, as though the bridge is at last "form'd," the "anchor" holding. A discussion of this poem will also necessarily get into Whitman's use of figurative language. Implicitly the speaker's soul is a noiseless, patient spider, "ceaselessly musing, ceaselessly venturing," building a "bridge" in the vastness (i.e., uniting the present with eternity?).

Part of the manuscript of Robert Frost's "Stopping by Woods" is printed in Charles W. Cooper and John Holmes, *Preface to Poetry*, with a fine essay by Holmes. Facsimile and essay are reprinted in Paul Engle and Warren Carrier, *Reading Modern Poetry*. Our first question calls attention to some of the manuscript readings. Others are: line 9, "She gives her" (for "He gives his"); line 12, "Fall of flake," (for "downy flake"); line 15, "That bid me give the reins a shake," deleted and replaced by "That bid me on, and there are miles" (which was also deleted). On "Stopping by Woods" see also John Lynen, *The Pastoral Art of Robert Frost*, and *Frost: Centennial Essays*, Jac L. Tharpe, ed. We number ourselves among the readers who see in the poem a longing for death ("frozen lake," "darkest evening of the year," "The woods are lovely, dark and deep" seem to support this view), but of course that is not what the poem is exclusively about. If there is a momentary longing for death in the poem, there is also the reassertion of the will to face the tasks of living.

On Keats's "Grecian Urn," see Harvey Lyon's casebook, *Keats's Well-Read Urn*. For a microscopic analysis of the poem, see Earl Wasserman, *The Finer Tone*. Among the newer lucid discussions of this poem are those in books on Keats by Walter Jackson Bate, Douglas Bush, and Aileen Ward. See also Helen Vendler's discussion in *Studies in Romanticism* 12 (1973), pp. 591-606. The instructor is reminded that Keats's "To Autumn" appears in Chapter 16 in *An Introduction to Literature*. Possibly some instructors will want to make use of Pound's "Immorality" (Chapter 14) or of Dylan Thomas's "Fern Hill" (Chapter 16).

Bertrand Bronson, *MLN* 63 (1948), points out that part of the fun in "When daisies pied" and "When icicles hang by the wall" is Shakespeare's "unexpected flouting of convention," for winter is presented -- with all of its discomforts -- as joyful (the country folk will drink cider and eat a stew within a hall heated by a log fire), and spring is, for all of its beauty, a time when the married man must fear that he will be cuckolded. Moreover, as Joseph Westlund points out in *Shakespeare Quarterly* 18 (1967), "When daisies pied" is far more abstract than is "When icicles hang by the wall"; in the former we get unnamed shepherds, whereas in the latter we get Dick (who blows his nails), Tom (who carries logs), greasy Joan, and red-nosed Marian. Still, there are also strong resemblances between the two songs. As C. L. Barber says in *Shakespeare's Festive Comedy* (p. 118):

> Each centers on vitality, and moves from nature to man. The spring song goes from lady smocks to the maidens' summer smocks, both showing white against the green of the season, from turtle cocks who "tread" to implications about people. The old joke about the cuckoo is made so delightful because its meaning as a "word," as a call to the woods, is assumed completely as a matter of course. In the winter song, the center of vitality is the fire. . . . The fire is enjoyed "nightly," after the day's encounter with the cold. Gathered together "When roasted crabs hiss in the bowl," it is merry to hear the owl outside in the cold -- his "Tu-whit, to-who" come to mean this moment. Even the kitchen wench, greasy Joan, keeling the pot to keep it from boiling over, is one of us, a figure of affection.

THE SPEAKING TONE OF VOICE

Reuben Brower in *The Fields of Light*, and also in his books on Pope and on Frost, has written excellently about this topic. Frost himself several times refers to the matter in *Selected Letters*, notably on page 107 ("The living part of a poem is the intonation entangled somehow in the syntax, idiom and meaning of a sentence"), pp. 110-11, p. 191.

Robert Langbaum also concerns himself with "voice," in *The Poetry of Experience*, which has a good analysis of Browning's "My Last Duchess." On this poem see also Laurence Perrine in *PMLA* 74 (March 1959), pp. 157-59. It may here be mentioned that although every poem has a "voice," not every poem needs to be a Browningesque dramatic monologue giving the reader a strong sense of place and audience. Tennyson's "Ulysses" (see the discussion below in the comments on Chapter 16) has been much criticized because the ostensible audience is not always strongly perceived, but no one would criticize Marvell's "To His Coy Mistress" (Chapter 13) on these grounds, though surely the "lady" addressed in line 2 gives place (in at least some degree) to a larger audience -- let us say a general audience -- when we get to "But at my back I always hear / Time's winged chariot hurrying near." On Herrick's "To the Virgins," see E. M. W. Tillyard in *The Metaphysicals and Milton*; Tillyard argues effectively that in "To the Virgins," "the trend of the poem is urgency, touched with reflection."

Among the good studies of satire are: James Sutherland, *English Satire*; Maynard Mack, "The Muse of Satire," *Yale Review* 41 (September 1951), pp. 80-92; and Robert C. Elliott, *The Power of Satire*. Edward W. Rosenheim interestingly suggests, in *Swift and the Satirist's Art*, that satire consists of an attack, clothed in fiction, upon "discernible historic particulars." It thus lies between polemical rhetoric (which usually lacks fiction), and, at the other extreme, comedy (which does not really attack, for it does not seek to change the reader's judgment). Among other satires in *An Introduction to Literature* (in addition to those included in this chapter) are Auden's "The Unknown Citizen" and Eliot's "The Love Song of J. Alfred Prufrock."

Herrick's "To the Virgins" shares the *carpe diem* theme with Marvell's "To His Coy Mistress," but as we try to point out on p. 64 of this manual, there are great differences. Students can be asked to compare the voices in the poems.

William Carlos Williams's "This Is Just to Say" pretends to be a note, perhaps left on the kitchen table or in the icebox. The space between the title (which is also the first line) and "I have eaten" may imitate the pause that the writer made -- one begins a note boldly and then after writing a couple of words one hesitates and wonders just how to put it -- or maybe it indicates the sort of pause that a reader makes while reading a scribbled note. As for the last two lines, by ending with "cold" rather than with "sweet" the poem becomes less sentimental, less predictable, and also probably more realistic, because the chief reason for eating fruit taken from the refrigerator is to experience the sensation of coldness, not sweetness.

Some critics applaud the neighbor in Frost's "Mending Wall," valuing his respect for barriers. For an extreme version, see Robert Hunting, "Who Needs Mending?" *Western Humanities Review* 17 (Winter 1963), pp. 88-89. The gist of this faction is that the neighbor wisely realizes -- as the speaker does not -- that individual identity depends on respect for boundaries. Such a view sees the poem as a Browningesque dramatic monologue like "My Last Duchess," in which the self-satisfied speaker unknowingly gives himself away.

Richard Poirier, in *Robert Frost*, makes the interesting point that it is not the neighbor (who believes that "good fences make good neighbors") who initiates the ritual of mending the wall; rather, it is the speaker: "I let my neighbor know beyond the hill." Poirier suggests that "if fences do not 'make good neighbors,' the *making* of fences can," for it makes for talk -- even though the neighbor is hopelessly taciturn. For a long, judicious discussion of the poem, see John C. Kemp, *Robert Frost: The Poet as Regionalist* (1979), pp. 13-25.

The first quatrain of Michael Drayton's "Since there's no help" (though it is joined to the next quatrain by a semicolon) is in effect a complete sentence. The speaker seems resolute, though perhaps in retrospect we feel that the repetition of "glad" in line 3 ("I am glad, yea, glad with all my heart") is a clue that insincerity causes him to protest too much. The second quatrain, which can also stand as a sentence, continues the matter-of-fact tone. But then, after the eighth line, comes the turn or *volta* so often found in sonnets. In the third quatrain and couplet -- this quatrain cannot stand as a

sentence, but passionately overflows into the couplet, and so
the quatrain and couplet together can be taken as a sort of
sestet -- we hear a new breathlessness or sense of urgency
that dispels the earlier apparent confidence. The abstractions,
too, are new (Passion, Faith, etc.); they do *not* indicate insincerity or lack of feeling, but, on the contrary, take us
into a world of bruised feelings, evident earlier in such an
expression as "you get no more of me." Even the shift from
"you" in line 2 to "thou" in line 13 is significant in establishing the change. The poem ends with a feminine rhyme,
probably to keep it from ending too emphatically, or, to put
the matter a bit differently, to indicate that the speaker is
not the master of the situation.

Ransom's "Piazza Piece" is a sonnet, and sonnets often treat
of love, but few if any others treat the old theme of "Death
and the Maiden": like all of the poems in this section, it
should be read aloud, and when it is read aloud the apparently
odd placement of "listen to an old man not at all" seems perfectly right, catching the old-fashioned tone of the suitor.

On Hopkins's "Spring and Fall," see Paul L. Mariani, *A Comen-
tary on the Complete Poems of Gerard Manley Hopkins*, and Peter
Milward's essay in Milward and R. V. Schoder, *Landscape and
Inscape*. If one wants to get into trouble, and wishes to talk
about sprung rhythm, one might first read Paull Baum in *PMLA*
74 (September 1959), 418-25. George Starbuck has a modern
version ("Translations from the English") in his book of poems,
White Paper.

Like many of Ted Hughes's other poems, "Hawk Roosting" celebrates the energy of nature, especially its egotistical aggres-
siveness. (For a different view, arguing that the poem is a
satire against aggressive, materialistic men, see Anne Williams
in *Explicator* 38 [Fall 1979], pp. 39-41.) If we compare this
poem with Tennyson's "The Eagle" (in Chapter 11), we get an
idea of the difference between Victorian and mid-twentieth-
century nature poetry. Although in *In Memoriam* Tennyson
speaks of "Nature red in tooth and claw," in "The Eagle" he
manages to sanitize his rapacious bird. We are told nothing
of the prey the eagle seizes, and the emphasis is on the bird's
grandeur: the bird lives among "mountain walls," and when he
plummets, he is "like a thunderbolt." And although Tennyson
uses personification, the bird is not sullied by any close resemblance to man. But Hughes's hawk seems to speak both with
the voice of Nature and the voice of rapacious man: "I sit on
top of the world"; "I kill where I please"; "No arguments
assert my right"; "I am going to keep things like this." If
this is menacing, it is also refreshingly honest.

Shelley's "Ozymandias" (in Chapter 13) goes well here, there being three voices in the poem: the narrator, who speaks the first line; the traveler, whose words are quoted; and the king, whose words the traveler quotes. Moreover, much of the force of "Ozymandias" comes from the fact that there is no direct denunciation of the king's pride. In Chapter 16, Eliot's "Prufrock" and "Journey of the Magi" are especially relevant to this chapter, but they are difficult and will take a good deal of class time if taught early in the term. Donne's poems go very well with Chapter 10.

Gray's "Ode on the Death of a Favorite Cat" is the subject of a good essay in Geoffrey Tillotson's *Augustan Studies*. Tillotson points out, among other things, that the cat's name, Selima, is that of the heroine in Rowe's *Fair Penitent*, and that Selima, gazing on the lake (lines 5-6) evokes Pope's Helen of Troy, gazing down from the walls upon the armed warriors: "Meantime the brightest of the female kind, / The matchless Helen o'er the walls reclined." The poem is also discussed in Irene Tayler, *Blake's Illustrations to the Poems of Gray*.

11

FIGURATIVE LANGUAGE: SIMILE, METAPHOR, PERSONIFICATION, APOSTROPHE

If the idea that metaphors are like riddles is appealing, ask the class why the camel is "the ship of the desert." They will soon see that the figure goes beyond saying that the camel is a means of transportation, for the figure brings out both the camel's resemblance (at a great distance) to a sailboat and the desert's resemblance to an ocean.

On figurative language consult Monroe Beardsley, *Aesthetics*; Isabel Hungerland, *Poetic Discourse*; W. K. Wimsatt, Jr., and Cleanth Brooks, *Literary Criticism*, pp. 749-50; and Terence Hawkes, *Metaphor*. Probably as good as any statement about figurative language is Shelley's, that the language of poets "is vitally metaphoric; that is, it marks the before unapprehended relations of things and perpetuates their apprehension." Such a view, of course, holds that poetry is a form of knowledge, and the instructor may wish to have the class make some use of Chapter 1, "Some Theories of Literature." On Waller's "Song" and Jarrell's "Death," see M. L. Rosenthal and A. J. Smith, *Exploring Poetry*.

Sylvia Plath's "Metaphors" is in nine lines of nine syllables each, a sort of joking reference to pregnancy, which is what this riddling poem is about.

In "On First Looking into Chapman's Homer," Keats uses figures to communicate to the reader the poet's state of mind. Figures of traveling (appropriate to a poem about the author of *The Iliad* and *The Odyssey*, and also, via "realms of gold" or El Dorado, to the Elizabethans) give way in the sestet to figures of exploration and discovery. (By the way, it is not quite right to say that at line 9 we pass from the octave's images of land to the sestet's images of discovery. An important shift occurs in line 7, with "Yet" no less important than line 9's "Then." "Breathe" in line 7 is probably transitional, linked to the octave's idea of foreign travel and also to the sestet's early reference to the skies.) Probably it is fair to say that the octave (as compared with the sestet) has a somewhat mechanical, academic quality. "Realms of gold," "goodly states," "bards in fealty to Apollo," "demesne," etc., all suggest something less than passionate utterance, a tone reinforced by the rather mechanical four pairs of lines, each pair ending with a substantial pause. But in the sestet the language is more concrete, the lines more fluid (it can be argued that only line 10 concludes with a pause), and the meter less regular, giving a sense of new excitement that of course corresponds to the meaning of the poem. Almost all critics agree Keats erred in giving Cortez for Balboa, but C. V. Wicker argues in *College English* 17 (April 1956), pp. 383-87 that Keats meant Cortez, for the point is not the first discovery of something previously unknown, but an individual's discovery for himself of what others have earlier discovered for themselves. Still, it seems evident that Keats slipped, and instructors may want to spend some class time discussing the problem of whether such a factual error weakens the poem.

We include Edmund Waller's elegant "Song" partly because we think that students will like it as much as we do. Students complain that this book is full of writings about death, and although this poem, too, is partly about death (of the rose, of the lady, of beauty), it is equally a celebration of life, for if it poignantly reminds us of the brevity of "all things rare," it also insists that they are to be enjoyed.

Robert Frost has said of "The Pasture":

> I have always had an interest in that word, "confusion." I don't think I really thought of it in this poem, but it could be thought of in connection with it. I wrote it a long time ago. I never had a greater pleasure than on coming on a neglected spring in a pasture in the woods. We clean out the leaves, then wait by to watch the uncloudiness displace the cloudiness. That is always a pleasure to me; it might be taken as a figure of speech. It is my place to see clarity come out of talk and confusion. You didn't need to know that was in the poem. But now you see that was the way it was used.

This passage is given in Daniel Smythe, *Robert Frost Speaks*, pp. 56-57. Frost's last book, *In the Clearing*, owes its name to a poem entitled "A Cabin in the Clearing," but line 3 of "The Pasture" perhaps exerted its influence too. Frost, having gone the promised miles, also went from a clouded spring to a clear one, as well as to a cleared part of the woods.

Roy Harvey Pearce, in *The Continuity of American Poetry*, p. 339, regards William Carlos Williams's "The Red Wheelbarrow" as sentimental (but of some value), and says that what "depends"

is the poet: "He assures himself that he is what he is by virtue of his power to collocate such objects into sharply anno-
tated images like these." Charles Altieri in *PMLA* 91 (1976),
p. 111, suggests that although the items are stripped of asso-
ciations, "No poem in English is more metonymic. Three objects
evoke a mode of life in the sparsest, most succinct manner possible. The poverty of detail, like that in the rural paintings
of Andrew Wyeth, at once intensifies the starkness of rural
life and exemplifies it." Altieri also points out that in each
of the last three stanzas, the first line "depends" on the
second, for the word that ends each first line is often a noun
("wheel," "rain," "white"), but in the poem turns out to be an
adjective. Thus the reader's mind "is made to hover over details until its waiting is rewarded, not only within the stanza,
but also as each independent stanza emerges to fill out this
waiting and to move us beyond details to a complex sense of a
total life contained in these objects." John Hollander (*Vision
and Resonance*, p. 111) suggests that cutting "wheelbarrow"
and "rainwater" (with no hyphens to indicate that "rain" and
"white" are parts of the compounds) helps to convey what the
poem is about: seeing the constituents of things in the fresh-
ness of light after rain.

Tennyson's concise account in "The Eagle" seems literal enough,
but of course from the first the bird is personified, by being
called "He" instead of "it," and by being given "hands" instead
of talons. Note also that "his mountain walls" implies that
the bird is lord of a fortress. "Wrinkled sea" and "crawls"
are other obvious figures, giving us the sea from a man-bird's
eye view. The simile "like a thunderbolt he falls" returns us
from the eagle's point of view to the observer's. "Ringed with
the azure world," we should mention, has been interpreted as
expressing the bird's view of the earth spread out in a circle
before him, but we assume that "azure" is proof that the description is not of the earth but of the sky around the bird,
and so the line is from an observer's point of view. Robert
Graves assaults the poem in *On Poetry: Collected Talks and
Essays*, pp. 402-05. Graves suggests that if the eagle's claws
are hands, when we are told that the eagle "stands" he must be
standing on his wings, and Graves claims that line 3 adds
nothing: "Since the eagle perches on his crag close to the
sun, a background of blue sky has already been presumed."
Graves goes on to complain that "lands" has been chosen for
the rhyme with "hands" and "stands," not for the sense, because "the eagle can stand only in one land." And "close to
the sun" is objectionable; "what," Graves asks, "are a few
hundred feet, compared with 92,000,000 miles!"

In Dickinson's "Because I could not stop for Death," the fact that a grave is suggested in lines 17-20 eludes many students; the reference to the grave contributes to toughening the poem. This stanza, by the way, is a good example of the closeness of some metaphors to riddles, a point discussed earlier in the chapter. Selections from a number of commentaries (including, among others, Allen Tate, *Reactionary Essays*; Yvor Winters, *In Defense of Reason*; and Richard Chase, *Emily Dickinson*) are collected in *Fourteen by Emily Dickinson*, ed. Thomas M. Davis. See also Clark Griffith, *The Long Shadow*, pp. 128-34.

Whoever first called a train an "iron horse" had the gift of the poet, but Dickinson goes much further in "I like to see it lap the Miles," catching the beast's energy and (in the last three lines) its docility. She is interested in the sound and sight of the train (these are playfully set forth with lots of alliteration, beginning with "like . . . lap . . . lick"), but she displays no interest in the train as a symbol of progress, no interest in people or goods getting anywhere. Indeed, her train ends up -- for all its rushing and roaring -- "At its own stable door."

Most critics, concentrating on the last third of William Carlos Williams's "The Yachts," insist that the poem is finally not about yachts but about the rich who acquire wealth and power by exploiting the "beaten, desolate" masses and who ignore the "cries" of those whom they victimize. Typical of such readings is this comment from Leonard Unger and William Van O'Connor, *Poems for Study* (1953), p. 10:

> The reader discovers that the sea and the waves are imagined to be masses of people who attempt to hold back the progress of the yachts. At this point the implication of the poem becomes clearer: the yachts are those who live well at the expense of vast numbers of people. Sometimes it is necessary for this small coterie to move a little more slowly, to take less advantage of other people than they would like to take; they are forced, as we say, to trim their sails a little, to "take in canvas." The symbolism of the slight, trim yachts overcoming the waves in the bay emphasizes the point that merely a few can overcome great masses of their fellows.

This is pretty crude; Howard Nemerov offers a much more subtle and more acceptable version of this interpretation in *Figures of Thought* (1978), when he says (page 162),

It is not so much that yachts and yacht-racing form
an allegory of the workings of society, in this instance a society based upon free enterprise capitalism, but that these institutions and their associated imagery are in themselves the making visible
of the beauty and the horror of a competition claimed
to be held under the laws of nature but where the
laws of nature are rigged in favor of great wealth.
. . . It is not necessary to make explicit the equa-
tion: yachts are, say, business enterprises, family
fortunes. They are yachts, and what is said of
them applies to yachts and yacht-racing; nevertheless what is said of them makes them stand forth as
symbolic of certain characteristics of the market-
place from which they come. . . . [Near the end of
the poem] the boats with their sharp prows cutting
the waters have by now developed by the poet's perception of them into a further metaphor representing
the pitiless and unequal warfare carried on by the
rich against the poor. To be "live with the grace
of all that in the mind is feckless [*sic*], free and
naturally to be desired" requires, alas, this cruel
corollary, that it can be done only by those who in-
flict massive sufferings on others and who remain
massively indifferent to these sufferings.

We think that even Nemerov's interpretation is too political,
and that, in a sense, it turns the poem inside-out. We take
the poem to be less qualified in its celebration of the yachts.
The turbulent water over which these "youthful," "rare,"
"fleckless" vessels sail is compared to "an entanglement of
watery bodies"; true, it is a bit odd to compare water to
watery bodies, but Williams is not the first poet to use an
unconventional figure. Moreover, he may here be influenced
by the famous painting of *The Great Wave* by Hokusai, where the
foam of the waves resembles clutching fingers; the wave is
both a wave and (almost) a collection of human hands grasping
upward out of the water. In any case, "beaten, desolate" personifies the waves, and need not turn our thoughts too strongly
to ideas of one class of people exploiting another. Put it
this way: the poet, through various figures of speech, is
helping us to see the *waves* (imagining them as people defeated
by grace and energy), not helping us to understand the nature
of free enterprise capitalism. Williams's imagination is
stimulated, not repelled, by the sight of the racing yachts,
and his mind moves from the yachts to the water, which at first
is imagined as resembling writhing hands, and then his imagination presents all of the bodies that the sea has engulfed.

In teaching the poem -- and for us "teaching" almost always
means reading the work aloud, and then rereading it, part by
part, with comments or questions interspersed -- we try to
call to the students' attention the matter-of-fact, almost im-
perceptible figures. Even the opening words -- "The Yachts
Contend" -- after all, are not quite literal; crews contend,
but yachts can't. Similarly, students can be directed to think
about "an ungoverned ocean which when it chooses / tortures the
biggest hulls," about "bellying sails," about "lesser and
greater craft which, sycophant, lumbering" follow the yachts,
and about a "mind that is fleckless."

Other points: (1) The first sentence is five lines long (i.e.,
it runs into the second stanza), the second sentence is seven
lines long, and the third sentence is five and a half. After
the middle of the poem, when the wind fails (line 21), the sentences are relatively short (lines 18-21), but once the race
begins we get some long lines again. (2) "Fleckless" in line
17 is the right word; some texts print "feckless" (following
an edition of Williams's poems that contained this misprint),
but when Williams read the poem he said "fleckless." (3) Williams apparently began writing the poem in *terza rima* but
abandoned the scheme in the middle of the second stanza.

Among the highly relevant poems in Chapter 16 are Donne's
"Valediction," Keats's "To Autumn," and Ginsberg's "A Supermarket in California." We briefly discuss, in the commentary
on "A Collection of Poems," the figures of speech in Shakespeare's Sonnet 29 ("When in disgrace"), a poem that goes very
well with this chapter. William Carlos Williams's "Spring and
All" is an interesting example of a poem with almost no figurative language -- until near the end.

(We reprint here a good explication, by a student, of Randall
Jarrell's "The Death of the Ball Turret Gunner.")

> Reading the first line aloud, one pauses slightly
> after "sleep," dividing the line in half. The halves
> make a sharp contrast. The point of transition in
> this line is "I fell," a helpless movement from the
> mother to the State, from sleep to the State. The
> mother and the State make an evident contrast, and
> so do "sleep" and "the State," which resemble each
> other in their first sound and in their position at
> the end of a half-line but which have such different
> associations, for sleep is comforting and the State
> is associated with totalitarianism. ("The country"
> or "the land" might be comforting and nourishing,
> but "the State" has no such warm suggestions.) We

will soon see in the poem that life in the "belly"
of the State is mindless and cold, a death-like life
which ends with a sudden and terrible death. A
mother, even in her "sleep," naturally protects and
nourishes the child in her warm womb; the State un-
naturally cramps the man in its icy belly. He
"hunched in its belly" until his "wet fur froze."
We gather from the title that "its" refers not only
to the State but also to the airplane in whose womb-
like ball turret he led his confined existence and
died. Given the title, the fur probably literally
refers to the fur lining of the jackets that fliers
wore in World War II, and it also suggests the
animal-like existence he led while confined by this
unfeeling foster parent, the State-airplane. His
unnatural existence is further emphasized by the
fact that, in the airplane, he was "Six miles from
earth." From such an existence, far from the "dream
of life" that people hope for, and still hunched in
the turret like a baby in the womb, he was born
again, that is, he awoke to (or became aware of) not
a rich fulfillment of the dream but a horrible reality that is like a nightmare. "Woke to black
flak" imitates, in its rattling k's at the ends of
words, the sound of the gunfire that simultaneously
awakened and killed him. His awakening or birth is
to a nightmarish reality and death. It is not sur-
prising, but it is certainly horrifying, that in
this world of an impersonal State that numbs and
destroys life, his body is flushed out of the turret
with a hose. This is the third horrible release:
the first was from the mother into the State; the
second was from the belly of the State into the
belly of the airplane; and now in shreds from the
belly of the airplane into nothing. That this
life-history is told flatly, with no note of protest, of course increases the horror. The simplicity of the last line more effectively brings
out the horror of the experience than an anguished
cry or an angry protest could do.

12

FIGURATIVE LANGUAGE: IMAGERY AND SYMBOLISM

For a discussion of the difference between *natural* symbols (items that are meaningful on the literal level but that mean much more too) and symbols that have no literal existence, such as a man who does not cast a shadow, see N. Friedman, "Symbol," in *Encyclopedia of Poetry and Poetics*, ed. Alex Preminger.

The references suggested for Chapter 11 are relevant here too. In addition, see Barbara Seward, *The Symbolic Rose*. Blake's "The Sick Rose" has been much interpreted, usually along the lines given in the text. (See Reuben Brower, *The Fields of Light*, and Rosenthal and Smith, *Exploring Poetry*.) But E. D. Hirsch, Jr., in *Innocence and Experience*, argues that "The rose is being satirized by Blake as well as being infected by the worm. Part of the rose's sickness is her ignorance of her disease. Her ignorance *is* her spiritual disease because in accepting 'dark secret love' she has unknowingly repressed and perverted her instinctive life, her 'bed of crimson joy.'" Hirsch argues his point for a couple of pages. Allen Ginsberg has "tuned" the poem (MGM Records FTS-3083).

Wallace Stevens's "Anecdote of the Jar" has also evoked controversy, chiefly on whether the jar is a symbol of man's superiority to nature, or a symbol of man's corruption of natural beauty. For a survey of various interpretations, see *College English* 26 (April 1965), pp. 527-32. William York Tindall, in *Wallace Stevens*, p. 24, argues that "the theme is interaction: the effect of the round jar on its surroundings and of them on it. This artifact composes nature, but not entirely; for the slovenly place still sprawls. Wilderness of bird and bush makes jar stand out, gray and bare." Frank Kermode, in *The Romantic Image*, dismisses the controversy over whether "the poet is *for* Nature or *for* Art." Kermode says:

> This is irrelevant, because the point of the jar's *difference*, and the manner of its difference, are what matters. It belongs to a different order of reality, already completely significant and orderly,

fixed and immortal. In one sense it is more vital,
in another sense less so, than the "slovenly wilderness" around it; the poem itself reconciles opposites by using the jar as a symbol . . . of what
moves in stillness, is dead in life, whose meaning
and being are the same.

See also Joseph N. Riddell, *The Clairvoyant Eye*, pp. 43-44,
and Harold Bloom, *Kabbalah and Criticism*.

On "The Emperor of Ice-Cream," first a comment by Stevens, in
a letter (*Letters of Wallace Stevens*, Holly Stevens, ed.) of
16 May 1945. He says of "concupiscent curds" that the words
"express the concupiscence of life, but, by contrast with the
things in relation to them in the poem, they express or accentuate life's destitution, and it is this that gives them something more than a cheap lustre" (p. 500).

If "emperor" suggests power and splendor, "ice cream" suggests
pleasure, especially sensuous enjoyment, triviality, and
transience. Put together, and in this context of a wake, the
implication is that man for a while shapes and enjoys the
tawdry world, as the dead woman embroidered fantails on her
sheets -- which were too short. We can take pleasure in the
world (there is certainly pleasure in the shifting diction and
in the alliteration in line 3, "In kitchen cups concupiscent
curds"), but if Stevens insists on the pleasure (cigars, ice
cream, flirting girls) he also insists on looking at ("Let the
lamp affix its beam") transience ("last month's newspapers,"
the dresser lacking knobs) and death (the corpse's horny feet).
The pleasures described, then, to return to Stevens's letter,
"accentuate life's destitution."

In another letter, published in *The Southern Review* (Autumn
1979), pp. 773-74, Stevens freely paraphrases part of the poem:
"let us have a respite from the imagination (men who are not
cigar makers, blondes, costumes, theology), and, in short,
suppose we have ice cream. Not that I wish to exalt ice cream
as an absolute good, although my little girl might. It is a
symbol, obviously and ironically, of the materialism or realism
proper to a refugee from the imagination." Stevens goes on,
however, to insist that "ambiguity [is] essential to poetry."

D. H. Lawrence's "Snake," a sort of dialogue between, on the
one hand, the "voice of my education" (which hates vitality
and danger) and, on the other hand, what Lawrence elsewhere
calls his "demon" (spontaneous self, which appreciates the
snake's elemental nature), can cause little difficulty, though
some students may miss the irony involved when the voice of

education says, "If you were a man / You would take a stick
and break him." The poem as a whole deflates this lifeless
view of manhood. But the poem is richly ambiguous, meta-
phorically suggestive of evil and perhaps also of the phallus,
and also (perhaps therefore) suggestive of power and vitality.

Among the interesting discussions of Coleridge's "Kubla Khan"
are Brooks and Warren, *Understanding Poetry*, 4th ed.; Humphry
House, *Coleridge*; Harold Bloom, *The Visionary Company*; and
Walter Jackson Bate, *Coleridge*. Most critics tend to see the
fountain, river, and chasm as symbols of the poet's consciousness, and "the pleasure dome" as a symbol of poetry. Charles
Patterson (*PMLA* 89 [October 1974], pp. 1033-42) believes that
the river (suggestive of poetic consciousness) is called
"sacred" because it is "given over to and seemingly possessed
by a god presenting through the poet's *furor divinus* a vision
of beauty." The "deep delight" of line 44 is, Patterson suggests, "a daemonic inspiration, an unrestricted and amoral joy
like that of the pre-Christian daemons." Patterson's judicious
article deserves close study. These days, since drugs are in,
the instructor may also wish to consult Elisabeth Schneider,
Coleridge, Opium, and Kubla Khan, or Alethea Hayter, *Opium and
the Romantic Imagination*. Apparently it is unsound to attribute
the poem to opium. As someone has said, Coleridge didn't write
"Kubla Khan" because he took opium; he took opium because he
was the sort of person who writes poems like "Kubla Khan."

In Chapter 16 Herrick's "Corinna" and Blake's "Lamb" and
"Tyger" are useful when talking about symbolism, as are Keats's
"La Belle Dame sans Merci" and Yeats's "Sailing to Byzantium."
Also appropriate is Whitman's "Out of the Cradle Endlessly
Rocking." In the words of Gay Wilson Allen, *A Reader's Guide
to Walt Whitman*, "Everything in the poem tends to be simile or
metaphor on the way to becoming symbols."

Suggested Topic for Writing:

"Kubla Khan" as a celebration of the energy of life. It can be
argued that even the references to ice and to the "sunless sea"
and "lifeless ocean" in this context suggest mystery rather
than lifelessness; certainly the Khan, the river, the fountain,
the dome, the wailing woman, and the poet (among other things)
combine to give a vision of a powerful and mysterious creativ-
ity.

13

IRONY AND PARADOX

The chapter itself refers to I. A. Richards's essay on irony;
reference may here be made to Cleanth Brooks's *The Well-Wrought
Urn*.

James Reeves, in *The Critical Sense*, does a hatchet job on
Shelley's "Ozymandias." (Ozymandias, incidentally, was the
name the Greeks used for Ramses II, the thirteenth-century
B.C. pharaoh who, like other pharaohs, built monuments to celebrate his own greatness. One such monument was a colossus
sixty feet tall, carved in stone by Memnon. Diodorus, a
Sicilian Greek historian of the first century, saw the statue
and wrote that it was inscribed, "I am Osymandyas, king of
kings; if any would know how great I am, and where I lie, let
him excel me in any of my works." At some later date the
statue tumbled, leaving only fragments.) Reeves's objections
include: "vast" (line 2) means "of great extent," but the legs
would be tall rather than vast; "in the sand" (line 3) is
hardly necessary after "in the desert"; if the visage is
"shattered" (which Reeves takes to mean "broken to pieces"),
it would be difficult to recognize the facial expression; the
speaker says that the sculptor "well . . . read" the subject's
passions, but we cannot know if this is true since we have
no other information about the subject; if it is argued that
the inscription is evidence of cold-hearted tyranny, the sestet should begin "For," not "And"; to speak of "the decay" of
a "wreck" is tautological; in lines 13-14 "boundless" makes
unnecessary "stretch far away," and "bare" makes "lone" unnecessary. Some of Reeves's objections are telling, some are
niggling; in any case, the power of the poem is chiefly in the
essential irony and the almost surrealistic scene of legs
arising in the desert, the face on the ground nearby, and no
trunk anywhere.

A small point: lines 4-8 are unclear, for it is not certain
if "the hand . . . and the heart" belong to the sculptor, in
which case the idea is that the sculptor "mocked" ("mimicked,"
"imitated in stone") the passions and "fed" them by creating
them in stone, or if the hand and the heart belong to

Ozymandias, whose hand mocked the passions of his foes and whose heart fed his own passions.

Shakespeare's Sonnet 146 is well discussed in Edward Hubler, *The Sense of Shakespeare's Sonnets*, and more learnedly and elaborately discussed by Michael West in *Shakespeare Quarterly* 25 (Winter 1974), pp. 109-22. Also useful is *A Casebook on Shakespeare's Sonnets*, Gerald Willen and Victor B. Reed, eds.

All his life the dead man in Stevie Smith's "Not Waving but Drowning" sent messages that were misunderstood. His efforts to mask his loneliness and depression were more successful than he intended. His friends mistook him for a "chap" who "always loved larking," as they now mistake the cause of his death. But true friends would have seen through the clowning, the dead man seems to protest, in lines 3 and 4 (when of course it is too late to protest or to explain). The second stanza confirms his view of the spectators. They are imperceptive and condescending; their understanding of the cause of his death is as superficial as their attention to him was while he was alive. But they didn't know him "all [his] life" (line 11). The dead man thus acknowledges, by leaving them out of the last stanza, that, never having risked honest behavior, he is at least as responsible as others for his failure to be loved and to love.

Ransom's "Bells for John Whiteside's Daughter" has been discussed in Brooks, Purser, and Warren, *An Approach to Literature*. (Substantially the same comment appears under Warren's name in *Kenyon Review* 5 [Spring 1943], pp. 238-40.)

Helen Vendler, in *The Poetry of George Herbert*, points out that "The Pulley" draws not only on the material creation of man in Genesis (with the difference that in the poem the Fall occurs in the creation) but also on the "psychological" creation story of Pandora, which tells how man, at first given all blessings, was allowed to keep only one, Hope. In Herbert's reversal of the Pandora story, man keeps all of the blessings except rest, and this version leads to a pun: man keeps the "rest" (i.e., the remainder) but is afflicted (blessedly) with "restlessness." Indeed, man is afflicted with "repining restlessness"; Vendler calls attention to "re-pining" (which can be *re* plus *pine* in two senses, to wither and to yearn). She calls attention also to the fact that "the apparent inhumanity of God, his strict adherence to an ideal of worship in the penultimate stanza," i.e., "Herbert's least appealing view of God" almost disappears, for chiefly we are left, at the end of the poem, with a view of God as welcoming not only those who come to Him through "goodness" but even those whom restlessness "may toss" to Him.

Marvell's "To His Coy Mistress" is well discussed by J. V. Cunningham, *Modern Philology* 51 (August 1953), pp. 33-41; by Francis Berry, *Poets' Grammar*; by Joan Hartwig in *College English* 25 (May 1964), pp. 572-75; and by Bruce King in *Southern Review* 5 (1969), pp. 689-703. Incidentally, "dew" in line 35 is an editor's emendation for "glew" in the first edition (1681). Grierson suggests "glew" means a shining gum found on some trees. Another editor, Margoulieth, conjectures "lew," i.e., warmth. Marvell's poem can be the subject of a paper involving a comparison with Herrick's "To the Virgins." Although both poems take as their theme the *carpe diem* motif, the tone and the imagery of the two poems differ greatly. For example, the sun in Herrick's poem ("the higher he's a-getting") does not race through the sky, but in Marvell's poem the lovers will force the sun to hurry. Or, again, in Herrick's poem the speaker is concerned not with satisfying his own desires but with the young women, whereas in Marvell's poem one strongly feels that the speaker is at least as concerned with himself as with the woman.

Donne's "The Flea" is discussed in a fine article by Patricia Spacks in *College English* 29 (1968), pp. 593-94. "The Flea," with the rest of Donne's *Songs and Sonnets*, has been edited by Theodore Redpath; the edition has much useful information, but this poem scarcely needs an editor's elucidation.

"Batter my heart" has been several times discussed in *Explicator* (March 1953, Item 31; December 1953, Item 18; April 1954, Item 36; October 1956, Item 2). In *College English* 24 (January 1963), pp. 299-302, John Parrish summarized these discussions, rejected the idea that in the first quatrain, especially in lines 2 and 4, God is compared to a tinker mending a damaged pewter vessel, and offered his own reading. All of these are conveniently reprinted in the Norton Critical Edition of *John Donne's Poetry*, A. L. Clements, ed. Our own winnowings from these essays follow. Although the first line introduces the "three-personed God," it is impossible to associate each quatrain with only one of the three persons. Still, the idea of the trinity is carried out in several ways: "knock, breathe, shine" becomes "break, blow, burn." And there are three chief conceits: God as a tinker repairing the damaged (by sin) speaker; the speaker as a town usurped by satanic forces; God as a forceful lover who must ravish the sinful speaker; or (lest one get uneasy at the thought that Donne presents himself as a woman) God as a lover who must fully possess the speaker's soul (the soul is customarily regarded as female). "O'erthrow" in the first quatrain, in line 3, leads to the image of the beseiged town in the second quatrain; "untrue" at the end of the second quatrain leads (because it can refer

to marital infidelity) to the conceit of the lover in the third
quatrain; and "ravish" in the final line can take us back to
"heart" in the first line of the poem. A useful, relatively
long explication by M. T. Wanninger appeared in *Explicator*
(December 1969), Item 37. M. H. Abrams, *Natural Supernatural-
ism*, pp. 50-51, points out that in "Batter my heart" Donne
draws on Revelation 21:5 ("Behold, I make all things new"),
and that "the ultimate marriage with the Bridegroom, repre-
sented as the rape of the longingly reluctant soul" draws on
"commonplaces of Christian devotion."

If Eliot's "Journey" (in Chapter 16) has not already been
taught, the instructor may wish to teach it at this point.
Also especially relevant is A. E. Housman's "To an Athlete
Dying Young."

RHYTHM
and
SOME PRINCIPLES OF VERSIFICATION

Paul Fussell, Jr.'s *Poetic Meter and Poetic Form* is a readable
discussion of metrics. Also of interest are Harvey Gross,
Sound and Form in Modern Poetry, and *Mid-Century Poets*, John
Ciardi, ed. (which includes useful comments by Wilbur, Roethke,
Jarrell, and others). More difficult, and much more special-
ized, is W. K. Wimsatt, Jr.'s "One Relation of Rhyme to Reason," in his *The Verbal Icon*.

A. E. Housman's "Eight O'Clock" is discussed by Rosenthal and
Smith, *Exploring Poetry*, and by Richard Wilbur, "Alfred Edward
Housman," *Anniversary Lectures 1959* (Library of Congress),
pp. 42-43. Wilbur points out that we learn almost nothing
about the condemned man -- not even what his crime was; we get
only the last half-minute of his life. A clock strikes eight,
the conventional hour for executions in England; to the victim, and to the reader, the clock seems to be some machine
that strikes down not merely hours but men. Note the ticking
in "clock collected," and the effect of the enjambment in the
seventh line, where the clock collects its strength and (after
a heavy pause) strikes the hour and ends the man's life. By
the way, the Library of Congress owns a notebook draft of the
poem, in which lines 3-4 run thus:

> One, two, three, four, on jail and square and people
> They dingled down.

Wilbur points out that the deletion of the reference to the
jail is a great improvement. "Suspense," he says, "requires
that the reason for the man's intent listening should not be
divulged until we come to the second stanza. Contrast requires too that the 'morning town,' as it is called in the
first stanza, be simply presented as a crowded market place
down to which the steeple clock almost gaily 'tosses' its
chiming quarters."

Williams's "The Dance" is in free verse, but the abundance of
dactyls (as in "Breughel's great picture," "dancers go round,"
"squeal and the blare") gives it a sort of stamping effect
appropriate to sturdy dancers wearing wooden shoes.

Writing of Roethke's "My Papa's Waltz" in *How Does a Poem Mean*, John Ciardi says that the poem seems to lack a "fulcrum" (Ciardi's word for a "point of balance" or point at which there is a twist in the thought, such as "Ah love" in line 29 of "Dover Beach") but that the fulcrum "occurs after the last line." In his terminology, "The fulcrum exists outside the poem, between the enacted experience and the silence that follows it."

We think it is a mistake to spend an hour discussing nothing but meter. It seems to us better to work some discussion of metrics into the daily meetings than to devote a meeting exclusively to this topic. The chapter is meant to provide a summary and a convenient dictionary, but instructors probably will already have made use of some of the material. For example, the instructor in teaching Keats's "On First Looking into Chapman's Homer" may already have mentioned (in commenting on the last line, "Silent, upon a peak in Darien") that when a line in a predominantly iambic poem begins with a trochaic adverb or adjective, "we often get [Paul Fussell notes in *Poetic Meter*, p. 65] a strong reinforcement of an effect of sudden quiet." Incidentally, a similar metrical effect occurs in Shakespeare's Sonnet 29 (printed in Chapter 16) where the ninth line (in effect the first line of the sestet) begins with a trochee ("Yet in"), marking the start of an energetic rejection of the depressed condition set forth in the octave.

One might at first think that a villanelle is an utterly inappropriate form in which to urge someone to "rage," but in Thomas's "Do not go gentle into that good night," addressed to a man on his deathbed, it proves appropriate because of its ritualistic, incantatory quality. In discussing the poem one can wonder why the night is "good." Probably because death is natural and inevitable (in line 4 "dark is right"), but surely too there is a pun on "good night" as an equivalent to death. Further, "the last wave" (line 7) is probably both a final wave of water (suggesting the last flow of life) and a final gesture of the hand; "Grave men" in line 13 of course alludes both to serious men and to men near the grave. Thomas's distinctions between "wise men," "good men," "wild men," and "grave men" have aroused various interpretations. W. Y. Tyndall, in *A Reader's Guide to Dylan Thomas*, suggests that wise men are philosophers, good men are moralists (perhaps Puritans), and wild men are "men of action and lovers of living." (He suggests that the grave men are poets.) M. W. Murphy, in *Explicator* 27, No. 6 (February 1970), Item 55, suggests that the wise men who preach wisdom are contrasted with the good men who live a life of wisdom. Both rage against death because they have accomplished nothing, the words of the former and the deeds of the latter having gone unheeded. The wild men are hedonists -- who at death discover they have not caught time -- and, in contrast to those Dionysian figures, the grave men are ascetic Apollonians who have missed the joys of life but who now, near the grave, see what they have missed. In short, for all men life is incomplete and too brief, and no one should "go gentle into that good night."

In presenting Robert Francis's "The Pitcher" to the class, ask if anyone knows the etymology of "eccentric" (cf. "eccentricity" in line 1). You may have to provide the answer yourself, but in any case you can explore with the students the ways in which a pitcher's art is "eccentricity."

Note that the first four stanzas do not rhyme, but they miss by only enough to "avoid the obvious" and to "vary the avoidance." "Aim" in line 1 comes as close as a word can to rhyming with "aim" in line 2, but the line drops off and misses by the merest fraction of a foot. And if obvious/avoidance and comprehended/misunderstood aren't strictly consonant, they are eccentrically so. No question about consonance or slant rhyme in "wild/willed." But perfect rhyme is reserved for the last couplet, which everyone (except the by now paralyzed batter) can see is a perfect strike. The rhyme scheme, the economical couplets, the tense but erratic repetitions in sentence structure, the eccentric placement of caesuras (in lines 4 and 9), all of course contribute to the poem's wit in imitating the performance it describes.

A COLLECTION OF POEMS

<u>William Shakespeare, Sonnets 29 and 73</u>. Shakespeare's sonnets have been masterfully edited in the Variorum Edition by Hyder Rollins, and have been interestingly discussed in Stephen Booth, *An Essay on Shakespeare's Sonnets*, and Hallett Smith, *Elizabethan Poetry*. Booth has good discussions of both of these sonnets; Smith discusses 73 as well as several sonnets that we do not print.

The rhyme scheme of Sonnet 29 is that of the usual Shakespearean sonnet, but the thought is organized more or less into an octave and a sestet, the transition being emphasized by the trochee at the beginning of line 9. The sense of energy is also communicated by the trochee that begins line 10, and yet another introducing line 11, this last one being especially important because by consonance and alliteration it communicates its own energy to the new image of joy ("Like to the lark"). As in most of Shakespeare's sonnets, the couplet is more or less a summary of what has preceded, but not in the same order: line 13 summarizes the third quatrain, line 14 looks back to (but now rejects) the earlier quatrains.

The first line surely glances at Shakespeare's unimpressive social position, and line 8 presumably refers to his work. Possibly the idea is that he most enjoyed his work before it became the source of his present discomfort. Edward Hubler, in *The Sense of Shakespeare's Sonnets*, notes that "the release from depression is expressed through the image of the lark, a remembrance of earlier days when the cares of his London career were unknown." To this it can be added that although the poem employs numerous figures of speech from the start (e.g., personification with "Fortune," synecdoche with "eyes" in line 1, metonymy with "heaven" in line 3), line 11, with the image of the lark, introduces the poem's first readily evident figure of speech, and it is also the most emphatic run-on line in the poem. Moreover, though heaven was "deaf" in line 3, in line 12 it presumably hears the lark singing "hymns at heaven's gate." "Sullen" in line 12 perhaps deserves some special comment too: (1) The earth is still somber in color, though the sky is bright. (2) Applied to human beings, it suggests the moody people who inhabit earth.

Sonnet 73 is chiefly a meditation on growing old, though the couplet relates this topic to the theme of love that is the subject of many of Shakespeare's sonnets. All three quatrains, in varying degrees, glance at increasing coldness and darkness, and each successive quatrain is concerned with a briefer period. In the first, the human life is compared to a year; in the second, to a day; in the third, to a few hours. In the first quatrain, there is a further comparison; the boughs of the autumnal trees are compared (in "bare ruined choirs") to the churches that had fallen into decay after England broke with Rome. Note, too, that it is reasonable to perceive, faintly, a resemblance between the shaking boughs and a trembling old person. The first quatrain, then, is rich in suggestions of ruined beauty and destroyed spirituality.

The second quatrain, by speaking of night as "Death's second self," explicitly introduces death into the poem. The third quatrain personifies the fire, speaking of its "youth" (i.e., the earlier minutes or hours of the blaze) and its "death-bed," and in its reference to ashes it introduces a common idea of the decayed body. (The idea, of course, is that the last embers lie on the ashes, which were the "youth" or earlier hours of the fire, and these ashes now help to extinguish the embers.) The year will renew itself, and the day will renew itself, but the firewood is utterly destroyed. In the final line the speaker is reduced to "that," not even "me."

John Donne, "A Valediction: Forbidding Mourning." See Theodore Redpath's edition of *The Songs and Sonnets of John Donne*, and see especially Clay Hunt, *Donne's Poetry*, and Patricia Spacks, *College English* 29 (1968), pp. 594-95. Louis Martz, *The Wit of Love*, p. 48, says of line 20: "'Care less,' but is it so? The very rigor and intricacy of the famous image of the compass at the end may be taken to suggest a rather desperate dialectical effort to control by logic and reason a situation almost beyond control."

Robert Herrick, "Corinna's Going A-Maying." See Cleanth Brooks, *The Well-Wrought Urn*.

John Milton, "When I consider how my light is spent." Milton's sonnets have been carefully edited by Ernst Honigmann (1966). Argument about the date Milton became blind need not concern

us (Miltonists wonder how literally to take "Ere half my days"),
but it should be noticed that one critic argues that the sonnet
is not about blindness. (The common title "On His Blindness"
has no authority; it was first used by a printer in 1752.)
Lysander Kemp held (*Hopkins Review* 6 [1952], pp. 80-83) that
the sonnet deals with the loss not of vision but of poetic inspiration, but Kemp's view has not been widely accepted. The
most sensible view (to draw on Honigmann) is that the octave
assumes that God requires ceaseless labor, and the sestet en-
larges the concept of service to include those who though in-
active are eagerly prepared for action. Additional notes: in
line 2, "this dark world and wide" suggests not only the dark
world of the blind man but is also a religious stock expression
for the sinful world; in line 7, "day-labor" suggests not only
labor for daily wages but also labor that requires daylight,
i.e., the power of vision; in line 14, "wait" perhaps means not
only "stay in expectation" but also "attend as a servant, to
receive orders."

William Blake, "The Lamb" and "The Tyger." E. D. Hirsch, Jr.,
Innocence and Experience, discusses these poems; Harold Bloom,
The Visionary Company, discusses "The Lamb," "The Tyger," and
"London." "The Tyger" has engendered much comment. Of special
interest are Martin K. Nurmi, "Blake's Revisions of 'The Ty-
ger,'" *PMLA* 71 (September 1956), pp. 669-85; Harold Bloom,
Blake's Apocalypse; and two pieces (by John Grant and by
Hazard Adams) reprinted in *Discussions of Blake*, John Grant,
ed.

Allen Ginsberg sings "The Lamb" on *Songs of Innocence and Experience by William Blake, Tuned by Allen Ginsberg* (MGM Records
FTS-3083).

William Blake, "London." "London," from *Songs of Experience*,
is a denunciation of the mind-forged manacles, i.e., of man-
made repressive situations, not a denunciation of cities with
a glorification of rural life. The church assists in exploi-
tation by promises of an eternal reward, the monarchy slaugh-
ters men for private gain, and marriage drives the unmarried
(or the unsatisfactorily married) to harlots. "Chartered"
(line 2), i.e., not merely mapped but licensed, is perhaps almost acceptable for streets, but that the river, an image of
freedom, should also be chartered is unnatural and intolerable.
As the poem develops, it is evident that children are licensed
(as chimney sweeps), soldiers are licensed (to kill and to be
killed), and harlots are licensed (bought and sold). E. D.
Hirsch, Jr., *Innocence and Experience*, suggests that there is
a further meaning: Englishmen were proud of their "chartered

liberties," rights guaranteed by Magna Carta, but "these chartered liberties are chartered slaveries." For "ban" in line 7 Hirsch offers four references: a summons to arms (king); a formal denunciation or curse (church); a proclamation of marriage; a prohibition (king, church, marriage). A few additional points: the church is "blackening" because (1) it is covered with the soot of an industrial (mechanistic) society; (2) it is spiritually corrupt; and (3) it corrupts people. The chimney-sweeper's cry appalls the church because the cry is a reproach, and "appalls" hints at "pall" (suggestive of the dead church) and at its literal meaning, "to make pale," i.e., the hypocritical church is a whited sepulcher. In line 14, "the youthful Harlot's curse" may be a cry (thus linked with the infant's cry, the chimney-sweeper's cry, and the soldier's sigh) or it may be the disease that afflicts her and is communicated to others. In an earlier version, "dirty" stood in lines 1 and 2 instead of "chartered," and "smites" instead of "blights" in line 16.

William Wordsworth, "Composed upon Westminster Bridge, September 3, 1802." Curiously, many students think that this sonnet describing the poet's response to the city at sunrise is a comparison between the city and the country, whereas in fact the poem suggests that city and country are united in "the beauty of the morning." City and country are personified (the city is said to "wear / The beauty of the morning," the houses "seem asleep"; the river has a "will"). (As Cleanth Brooks points out, in *The Well-Wrought Urn*, to say that the houses are "asleep" is to consider them not mechanical or dead but alive.) The only thing moving in the city is, paradoxically, the Thames (line 12) -- a perfect image of movement and stillness at once. The poem, then, is largely about the natural beauty of the city: the first line announces a thesis, the next seems to attack, rather rudely, anyone who might disagree with him, but perhaps the attack is not rude because perhaps Wordsworth is really speaking to himself, i.e., in effect saying "I would indeed be only a fool if I could not see beauty here as well as in my usual rural subjects." (In fact, he does seem to be referring to himself, defending himself against Charles Lamb's comment, in a letter, that Wordsworth probably was unfamiliar with urban emotions.) The remainder of the poem is a sort of demonstration of the proposition expressed in the first line. Small point: when a reader objected to the paradox of a city clothed in bareness, Wordsworth almost substituted a crown of beauty for the garment, but he explained his original imagery: "bare, as not being covered with smoke or vapor; -- clothed, as being attired in the beams of the morning."

William Wordsworth, "I Wandered Lonely as a Cloud." On 15
April 1802, William Wordsworth and his sister, Dorothy, took
a walk, during which they saw some daffodils near a lake.
Dorothy recorded the experience in her journal, and this entry
affords us something close to the raw material out of which
Wordsworth's poem was made. The entry is not, of course,
Wordsworth's own experience; Dorothy's experience was not
William's, and Dorothy's words cannot exactly reproduce even
her own experience. (It should be noted, incidentally, that
Dorothy's description is not entirely "factual"; her daffodils
rest their heads, glance, dance, etc.) Still, the entry gives
us something of the phenomena that stirred an emotion in Wordsworth, and for Wordsworth poetry was made out of "emotion recollected in tranquillity." Below is the entry from Dorothy's
journal. (We sometimes mimeograph the entry and ask the students to discuss the poem in the light of the entry.)

> It was a threatening, misty morning, but mild. We
> set off after dinner from Eusemere. Mrs. Clarkson
> went a short way with us, but turned back. The
> wind was furious, and we thought we must have re-
> turned. We first rested in the large boat-house,
> then under a furze bush opposite Mr. Clarkson's.
> Saw the plough going in the field. The wind seized
> our breath. The Lake was rough. . . . When we were
> in the woods beyond Gowbarrow Park we saw a few
> daffodils close to the water-side. We fancied that
> the lake had floated the seeds ashore, and that the
> little colony had so sprung up. But as we went
> along there were more and yet more; and at last,
> under the boughs of the trees, we saw that there
> was a long belt of them along the shore, about the
> breadth of a country turnpike road. I never saw
> daffodils so beautiful. They grew among the
> mossy stones about and about them; some rested
> their heads upon these stones as on a pillow for
> weariness; and the rest tossed and reeled and
> danced, and seemed as if they verily laughed with
> the wind, that blew upon them over the lake; they
> looked so gay, ever glancing, ever changing. This
> wind blew directly over the lake to them. There
> was here and there a little knot and a few strag-
> glers a few yards higher up; but they were so few
> as not to disturb the simplicity, unity, and life
> of that one busy highway. We rested again and
> again. The bays were stormy, and we heard the
> waves at different distances, and in the middle
> of the water, like the sea. Rain came on -- we
> were wet when we reached Luff's, but we called
> in.

Two years after the walk, William presumably recollected and contemplated the emotion, and wrote "I Wandered Lonely as a Cloud," leaving out the threatening weather, the plough, the boat, the miscellaneous flowers and even the first group of daffodils, and the people (including Dorothy). Notice, too, that the sense of effort which Dorothy records ("we thought we must have returned," "we first rested," etc.) is not in the poem: the speaker "wandered," and he lies on his couch in "vacant or in pensive mood"; if he acts, it is with spontaneous joy, but chiefly it is the daffodils that act ("fluttering and dancing in the breeze," "tossing their sprightly heads," etc.).

Wordsworth first published the poem in 1807, but the version printed here (which is the one everyone knows) is that of 1815. The differences between the first and second versions are these: in the first version lines 7-12 are lacking; line 4 has "dancing" instead of "golden"; line 5 has "Along" instead of "Beside"; line 6 has "Ten thousand" instead of "Fluttering and"; and line 16 has "laughing" instead of "jocund."

On Dorothy Wordsworth's *Journals* and William Wordsworth's "I Wandered Lonely as a Cloud," see Carl Woodring, *Wordsworth*; Edward Rosenheim, *What Happens in Literature*; David Perkins, *Wordsworth*, and especially Frederick Pottle's essay in *Yale Review* 40 (Autumn 1950), pp. 27-42, reprinted in *Wordsworth*, Gilbert T. Dunklin, ed.

John Keats, "La Belle Dame sans Merci." The poem is elaborately discussed in Earl Wasserman, *The Finer Tone*, and more reasonably discussed in books on Keats by Walter Jackson Bate and Douglas Bush, and in Harold Bloom, *The Visionary Company*. Here are a few points: In the first stanza, nature ("withered") reflects the condition of the knight ("*palely* loitering"). The second stanza further establishes the time as autumn, and though nature is abundant ("The squirrel's granary is full") the knight seems starved, and the implication is that he is approaching winter, i.e., death. Line 22 ("And nothing else saw all day long") indicates his total absorption in the lady's song, which (along with "roots of relish sweet, / And honey wild, and manna dew") nourished him for a while, and brought him to a vision of people who resemble him in his present condition ("pale"). This vision is presumably a vision of mortality, and he awakens to find himself "On the cold hill's side," i.e., in the physical world unredeemed by the imagination.

John Keats, "To Autumn." The poem is discussed in books on Keats by Walter Jackson Bate and by Douglas Bush, and also in Reuben Brower, *The Fields of Light*; see also Helen Vendler in *Studies in Romanticism* 12 (1973), 591–606. For an illuminating discussion of Keats and Wallace Stevens, see Vendler's "Stevens and Keats's 'To Autumn,'" in her *Part of Nature, Part of Us.* Some gleanings: One can see, in the three stanzas, the progress of autumn, from the first stanza with its "apples" and "mellow fruitfulness" before the harvest to the "half-reaped furrow" and the cider-press in the second stanza, and then the "stubble pains" in the third. One can perhaps also see the progress of a single day: the "maturing sun" of the first stanza may suggest noon; the resting figure of the second suggests mid-afternoon; and then "the last oozings hours by hours" suggest late afternoon; and of course the third stanza explicitly indicates the end of the day, by "soft-dying day" and "gathering swallows." There is also a movement from the cottage garden with its fruit trees and flowers in the first stanza to the granary, cider press, and fields of a farm in the second, and then to the hills and skies (though including the "garden-croft") of the third.

Alfred, Lord Tennyson, "Ulysses." Robert Langbaum, in *The Poetry of Experience*, and Christopher Ricks, in *Tennyson*, offer some good remarks; Paull Baum, in *Tennyson Sixty Years After*, assaults the poem. Henry Kozicki, in *Tennyson and Clio* (a book on Tennyson's philosophy of history), argues that "Ulysses" reveals Tennyson's optimism about historical progress and his despair about the role of a hero. For a review of much that should not have been written, see L. K. Hughes in *Victorian Poetry* 17 (Autumn 1979), 192–203. By the way, it is worth mentioning to students that Homer's hero wanted to get home, Sophocles's (in *Philoctetes*) is a shifty politician (as is Shakespeare's), and Dante's Ulysses (*Inferno* XXVI) is an inspiring but deceitful talker whose ardent search is for *forbidden* things.

The first five lines emphasize, mostly with monosyllables, the dull world Ulysses is leaving. With line 6 ("I cannot rest from travel") we see a rather romantic hero, questing for experience, and indeed "experience" is mentioned in line 19, but it must be added that something is done in the poem to give "experience" a social context: Ulysses has fought for Troy (line 17), he wishes to be of "use" (line 23), and he wishes to do "some work of noble note" (line 52). Lines 22–23 apparently say the same thing four times over, but readers are not likely to wish that Tennyson had deleted the superbly appropriate metaphor of the rusting sword. "Gray spirit" (line 30)

and "sinking star" (line 31) help (along with the heavy pauses
and monosyllables in lines 55-56) to define the poem as a
piece about dying, though students on first reading are likely
to see only the affirmations. Even the strong affirmations
in 57 ff. are undercut by "sunset" (line 60), "western" (61),
etc. But the last line, with its regular accents on the
meaningful words, affords a strong ending; perhaps the line
is so strong and regular that it is a bit too easy. In line
45 Ulysses directly addresses the mariners, yet we hardly sense
an audience as we do in Browning's dramatic monologues. If he
is addressing the mariners, who are aboard, where is he when
he refers to "this still hearth" (line 2) and when he says
"This is my son" (line 33)?

Suggested Topics for Writing:

1. Ulysses's voice.
2. Ulysses: hero or suicidal egotist?
3. Ulysses as he sees himself, compared with Ulysses as we
   see him.

Robert Browning, "Porphyria's Lover." Compared with "My Last
Duchess," this poem has more story and less of the diction of
a particular speaker, but students can fairly soon see that
the interest in "Porphyria's Lover" is not only in what happened but also in the speaker's mind. His insane egotism led
him to attempt to preserve forever Porphyria's love for him.
He believes that, although she struggles to offer her love,
her weakness (lines 21-25) made her require his assistance.
(Interestingly, in lines 6-15 she seemed energetic and efficient; perhaps there is even something a bit too efficient in
making the fire before speaking to her lover.) But his egotism is tempered with solicitude (lines 41-42, 50-54), making
him less monstrous but certainly mad. Inevitably, discussion
in class centers on the lover's motives (do we believe them?),
but it is useful to spend some time on the question of why
readers enjoy the story of a mad strangler.

Robert Browning, "Soliloquy of a Spanish Cloister." Because
the speaker of "Soliloquy" is soliloquizing rather than addressing someone, technically the poem is not a dramatic monologue. Still the poem is Browningesque; as in Browning's
dramatic monologues, the speaker reveals himself; here, although the monk is soliloquizing about Brother Lawrence, we
learn more about the speaker (he begins and ends with a growl)
than we do about his ostensible subject. For example, note
that his condemnation of Brother Lawrence's interest in "brown

Dolores" (stanza 5) really tells us only that the speaker lusts
for her. The malicious speaker, of course, though filled with
hatred, is proud of his pious adherence to mealtime rituals
(stanza 5), and he can, at the end, mechanically pray to the
Virgin although his mind is obsessed by his hatred of Brother
Lawrence.

If you are insatiably interested in the possible sources of
line 70 ("Hy, Zy, Hine"), you will want to consult *Victorian
Poetry* 17 (Winter 1979), pp. 377-83.

Walt Whitman, "Out of the Cradle Endlessly Rocking." There
are useful accounts by James E. Miller, Jr., *A Critical Guide
to "Leaves of Grass,"* and by Stephen E. Whicher in *Studies in
Romanticism* 1 (Autumn 1961), pp. 9-28. Whicher's important
essay is reprinted in *Walt Whitman,* Arthur Golden, ed., and in
The Presence of Walt Whitman, R. W. B. Lewis, ed., which also
contains three other essays on the poem. In the poem the
mature poet recreates the childhood experience that awakened
the poet in him. Lines 1-22 -- a single sentence telling how
the boy left his bed at midnight and wandered by the restless
seashore, and how he learned of love and death -- have been
called "oceanic" in their rhythm; in any case, they are a sort
of prologue, distancing the rest of the poem (the speaker is
"A man, yet by these tears a little boy again"), but, as
Whicher points out, of course the boyhood experience is presented for what it means to the man now. At the end of the
poem we are reminded that the experience is not of the present
but is a memory. Still, as we read we feel that the abundant
memories have taken possession of the man, almost overpowering
his will. The poem tells of the speaker's awakening to the
meaning of life (love) and to his destiny as a poet. The
bird's song stimulates awareness of love, and the boy-man dedi-
cates himself ("My own songs awakened from that hour"). The
boy wanders in colorful Paumanok (Long Island) in an atmosphere
of "lilac-scent," light, warmth, fertility (spring, the wedded
birds and the four eggs), and joy. Then, when the female bird
is missed, the boy becomes troubled; the male bird sings of
"lonesome love," and the scene changes from day to night.
(Again, the boy's perceptions are fused with the mature man's
understanding of the boy's experience.) The ocean sings of
death, and so the boy has experienced a double awakening: love
is inherently unsatisfied, and love and death are one. (Thus
Whicher.) But the poem never explicitly states any such meaning. As Miller points out, the reader, like the boy in the
poem, lives the experience and through the experience comes
intuitively to know.

Suggested Topics for Writing:

1. The unity of dualities (e.g., the crone rocking the cradle, the boy and the man, water and land -- blended in the seashore -- light and dark, life and death, material and spiritual).
2. The development of the musical imagery.
3. The stages in the boy-poet's development.

Matthew Arnold, "Dover Beach." "Dover Beach" begins with the literal -- the scene that hits the eye and ear -- moves in the second stanza to Sophocles's figurative tragic interpretation, in the third to Arnold's figurative religious interpretation, and finally -- the image of the sea now being abandoned -- to the metaphor of the world as a "darkling plain," whose only reality is the speaker and the person addressed. The end thus completes the idea of illusion versus reality that began in the first stanza, where the scene that was "tranquil" (line 5) actually contained the discords implicit in "grating roar," "fling," etc. For a sensitive reading of "Dover Beach," consult A. Dwight Culler, *Imaginative Reason: The Poetry of Matthew Arnold*. Finally, we call attention to Anthony Hecht's "Dover Bitch," printed later in this chapter. For parodies of modern critical methods, see Theodore Morrison in *Harper's Magazine* 180 (February 1940), pp. 235-44, where "Dover Beach" serves as grist for critics' mills.

Suggested Topic for Writing:

Is there a connection between the imagery of the sea in the first three stanzas and the imagery of darkness in the last stanza?

Emily Dickinson, "A narrow Fellow in the Grass." "Fellow" (and the pronouns "Him" and "His," rather than "it" and "its") and "rides" in the first stanza help to assimilate the snake to the human world, as do "comb" in the second stanza and "acre" in the third. In the fourth stanza the reference to a whiplash introduces a more threatening note; "Nature's People" in the next stanza seems to bring us back to the comfortable world of the first stanza, but with the last line of the poem ("Zero at the Bone") there is communicated a terror that indicates a response to the snake as supremely hostile. (The snake is, after all, a traditional image of man's satanic enemy.) The contrast between "a transport / Of cordiality" (which carries a sense of warmth, via *cor*, heart) and the coldness of "Zero at the Bone" could hardly be greater.

Karl Keller, in a provocative book about Emily Dickinson, *The Only Kangaroo among the Beauty*, says (p. 268) that the poem "manages to make Freud trite." Keller says that Dickinson's "tighter breathing / And Zero at the Bone" indicate that "she finds her genitals alarmed," and that "she is shocked and attracted by the male erection ('His notice sudden is')." He patently misreads the poem when he says, "Her own sexual desires are, she says, very strongly aroused; she feels 'a transport / Of cordiality.'" But of course the poem says that for "Several of Nature's People" she feels this transport, "*but*" for this fellow she feels "Zero at the Bone."

Dickinson complained when the third line was printed with a question mark at its end. Apparently "did you not" is less a question than a tagged-on conversational filler like "you know," and a question mark causes too long and too strong a pause. Yet another point about the punctuation: Lines 11-16, describing the boy (the speaker is a boy, not Emily Dickinson), stooping to pick up what he thinks is a whiplash but what is in fact a snake that disappears, are unpunctuated (until the end of line 16), and thus suggestive of the speed of the event.

Emily Dickinson, "I heard a Fly buzz when I died." Dickinson's poem juxtaposes some conventional religious images ("that last Onset," "the King," "What portion of me be / Assignable") with the buzz of a fly, rather than with, say, choirs of angels, and so, as Charles R. Anderson suggests in *Emily Dickinson's Poetry*, "the King witnessed in his power is physical death, not God." Should one go further, and suggest that Death-as-fly equals putrefaction? The last line of the poem ("I could not see to see") especially has attracted attention. Gerhard Friedrich (*Explicator* 13 [April 1955], Item 35) paraphrases it thus: "Waylaid by irrelevant, tangible, finite objects of little importance, I was no longer capable of that deeper perception which would clearly reveal to me the infinite spiritual reality." The fall into skepticism, Friedrich says, demonstrates the inadequacy of the earlier pseudo-stoicism. John Ciardi took issue with this interpretation and suggested (*Explicator* 14 [January 1956], Item 22) that the fly is "the last kiss of the world, the last buzz from life," reflecting "Emily's tremendous attachment to the physical world"; the final line, in his view, simply means "And then there was no more of me, and nothing to see with."

The Todd-Higginson editions gave "round my form" for "in the Room" (line 2), and "The eyes beside" for "The Eyes around" (line 5), "sure" for "firm" (line 6), "witnessed in his power" for "witnessed--in the Room" (line 8), and "What portion of

me I / Could make assignable--and then" for "What portion of
me be / Assignable--and then it was" (lines 10-11). It is
worth discussing with students the differences these changes
make.

Thomas Hardy, "Ah, Are You Digging on My Grave?" The narrative structure, as well as the motif of the unquiet grave (see
the ballad of that title in Albert B. Friedman's The Penguin
Book of Ballads) of course derives from traditional ballads.

Also ballad-like is the use of clichés or stock epithets (e.g.,
"My loved one," "My nearest, dearest kin"), but note that the
chief cliché of thought -- the next-to-last stanza, with its
stock idea of animal fidelity -- is offered only so that it
may be debunked in the final stanza.

It is worth asking students if -- were the author of this poem
not named -- they would take it to be a genuine traditional
ballad rather than a literary derivative. It is also worth
discussing Samuel Hynes's contention (*The Pattern of Hardy's
Poetry*, p. 53) that the poem -- based on the idea that no
affection survives death -- is neither true (as Hardy's own
poems to his dead wife demonstrate) nor effective (Hynes finds
the poem's irony "gross and automatic," "clumsy and cynical").

Thomas Hardy, "During Wind and Rain." The poem is not a dialogue, but there are nevertheless two voices here, a narrative
and a lyric one. The narrative voice utters the first five
lines of each stanza; the lyric voice utters the last two of
each stanza, beginning each of its utterances with "Ah, no."
The happy little narrative of people singing "their dearest
songs," "making the pathways neat," "blithely breakfasting,"
moving "to a high new house" -- presumably telling of the
lives of these people *as they see themselves* -- is undercut
in the last two lines of each stanza by a voice that speaks
more truly, seeing the inevitable decay: "the sick leaves reel
down in throngs," "the white stormbirds wing across" the neat
(but temporary) pathways and gardens, "the rotten rose is
ripped from the wall," and, finally, "Down their carved names
the raindrop plows." Only in the last stanza is the last word
a verb, and its position as well as its meaning gives it great
impact: the very names on the gravestones will be eradicated
even as the people themselves will be; the happy family will
return to the earth and (presumably) the earth will bring
forth new families who will go through the same cycle.

Thomas Hardy, "The Convergence of the Twain." The biggest and
perhaps the most luxurious ship ever built up to that time,
the supposedly unsinkable *Titanic* (it had sixteen watertight
compartments) collided with an iceberg and sank in the Atlantic
on 15 April 1912, during her maiden voyage from Southampton to
New York, with a loss of 1513 lives. Many of those who were
drowned were rich and famous.

Hardy completed the poem on 24 April 1912. He lost two acquaintances in the wreck, but the poem is not an elegy; rather
it is a sort of narrative and philosophical lyric which tells
of the destruction (fashioned by "the Immanent Will") that
awaits "the Pride of Life." The poem contains eleven stanzas,
the first five of which describe the "vaingloriousness" that
rests at the bottom of the sea, "Deep from human vanity"; the
next five (beginning with an emphatic transition, "Well") introduce the "Shape of Ice" and tell of "the intimate welding"
of ship and iceberg. (Note that "welding" -- which almost
sounds like "wedding" -- leads in the last line to "consumma-
tion"; the ship [female] at last meets her "mate.") The first
two lines -- notably brief -- of stanzas 2, 3, 4, and 5 call
attention to pride ("mirrors meant / To glass the opulent,"
etc.) and the last line -- notably long and sonorous -- of
each of these stanzas calls attention to the humbling of pride
("The sea-worm crawls," etc.).

Gerard Manley Hopkins, "God's Grandeur." "Charged" in line 1
is a scientific term (referring to electricity), leading to
"flame out" in the next line; "foil" in line 2, Hopkins explained in a letter, refers to "foil in its sense of leaf or
tinsel." Most of the first quatrain asserts the grandeur of
God, whose divine energy may be manifested either suddenly
("flame out") or slowly ("ooze of oil / Crushed"). "Crushed,"
at the beginning of line 4, is part of this celebration
(probably alluding to olives or seeds), but this word itself
of course also suggests destruction, and the rest of the octave is about man's corruption of himself and of nature.
"Man's smudge" in line 7 probably alludes to original sin as
well as to the destruction wreaked on the countryside by fac-
tories. The octave thus moves from an excited or urgent proclamation of God's grandeur to a melancholy reflection on man's
insensitivity to this grandeur. The sestet reintroduces a
joyous affirmation of God's grandeur. Lines 13 and 14 allude
to the traditional representation of the Holy Ghost as a dove,
but of course Christ is here seen also as the dawning sun,
giving warmth and light; "bent world" probably evokes the
curvature of the horizon, the world distorted by sin, and perhaps backbreaking labor. Paul L. Mariani, in his excellent

Commentary on the Complete Poems of Gerard Manley Hopkins, suggests that the last lines are connected with the first quatrain: "If we can picture the dawning sun before it breaks over the horizon, we may recall how the rich light seems precisely to 'gather to a greatness' in density and brightness . . . until the orb of the sun itself seems to spring forth, and then the sun flames out in strong rays like wings from its center." W. H. Gardner, in *Gerard Manley Hopkins*, vol. II, p. 230, suggests that the obvious meaning of the poem is that the world is a reservoir of Divine power, love, and beauty, and that the deeper meaning is that life must be jarred before the presence of God can be felt. On "verbal resonance" and other sound effects in the poem, see Brooks and Warren, *Understanding Poetry*, 4th ed., pp. 538-40. See also Terry Eagleton in *Essays in Criticism* 23 (1973), 68-75. Students might be invited to compare the poem with this entry (8 December 1881) from one of Hopkins's notebooks, reprinted in *The Sermons . . . of . . . Hopkins*, Christopher Devlin, ed., p. 95: "All things therefore are charged with love; are charged with God and if we know how to touch them give off sparks and take fire, yield drops and flow, ring and tell of him."

Gerard Manley Hopkins, "Spring." This poem is relatively simple, as Hopkins's poems go. The octave is filled with energetic verbs ("shoot," "rinse and wring," "strikes," "brush," "racing"), and several nouns also suggest activity ("rush," "fling"). Note, too, that "leaves and blooms" (line 6) are simultaneously nouns and verbs, and there are puns on "timber" (timbre) and "wring" (ring) in line 4. The sestet offers a Christian interpretation. The gist of the last four lines probably should be read in two ways: (1) Oh, Christ, get the innocent mind in the young before it clouds and sours, for they, Mary's son, are (since they are unfallen) most worthy of winning; (2) Innocence in the young, get Christ before your innocence sours from sinning, for He is most worthy of winning.

An instructor may wish to teach this poem along with other "spring" poems in this book: Shakespeare's "When daisies pied," William Carlos Williams's "Spring and All," and Dave Smith's "The Spring Poem."

A. E. Housman, *Shropshire Lad* #19 ("To an Athlete Dying Young"). Brooks and Warren, *Understanding Poetry*, 4th ed., print two manuscript versions of the poem, the first a very incomplete sketch, the second a rather full one.

A. E. Housman, "Loveliest of trees, the cherry now." If *carpe diem* poems on the surface seem to celebrate beauty and joy, they also -- by their emphasis on the brevity of these things -- usually introduce a note of sadness. In Housman's poem, the joy in perceiving the "loveliest of trees" at its loveliest moment (when in bloom) is somewhat undercut -- though more comically than pathetically -- by the speaker's assertion that he has "only" fifty years ahead of him. Certainly the speaker does *not* dwell on the pathos: the last stanza tells us that (since "fifty springs are little room") he is up and doing.

Curiously, "snow" in the last line has caused some readers to assert that the speaker is looking at cherry trees in the wintertime, presumably because fifty springs do not afford ample time for the experience of looking at the trees. But surely the first stanza tells us unambiguously that the tree is "hung with bloom" and that the season is Easter, i.e., the time of year when cherry trees in fact come into bloom. "Snow," in the last stanza, then, is a metaphoric way of describing the blossoms. But, of course, the metaphor *does* introduce the idea of winter and therefore of death; the poem emphasizes the beauty of spring -- at the very end -- by reminding us of winter, the end of the year, and by implication the end of life.

William Butler Yeats, "Leda and the Swan." On Yeats's "Leda" see Richard Ellmann, *The Identity of Yeats*, which includes three earlier manuscript versions. Also useful for discussion of "Leda" are Leo Spitzer's essay in *Modern Philology* 51 (May 1954), pp. 271-76; the comment in M. L. Rosenthal and A. J. Smith, *Exploring Poetry*; and Helen Vendler's fifth chapter in her *Yeats's Vision and the Later Plays*. Among Vendler's points are these: (1) the question at the end -- no mere rhetorical question -- represents a remarkable departure from the sestet of the traditional sonnet, which customarily has a neat unity; (2) although in the octave Leda is assaulted or caught, she is "caught up," enraptured, in the sestet. Her thighs are "loosening," not "loosened," and she feels the "heartbeat" and she senses the "glory" of her attacker; (3) Leda presumably does not acquire all of Jove's knowledge, but she does have a glimpse of divinity that is ordinarily unavailable.

Yeats saw political significance in the myth of beauty and war engendered by a god, but, as he tells us, when he was composing "Leda and the Swan" the political significance evaporated:

> After the individualistic, demagogic movements, founded
> by Hobbes and popularized by the Encyclopaedists and

the French Revolution, we have a soil so exhausted
that it cannot grow that crop again for centuries.
Then I thought "Nothing is now possible but some
movement, or birth from above, preceded by some
violent annunciation." My fancy began to play with
Leda and the Swan for metaphor, and I began this
poem, but as I wrote, bird and lady took such possession of the scene that all politics went out of
it.

William Butler Yeats, "Sailing to Byzantium." The literature
on "Sailing to Byzantium" is enormous. Among the readable
pieces are M. L. Rosenthal and A. J. Smith, *Exploring Poetry*;
and Elder Olson in *University Review* 8 (Spring 1942), pp. 209-
19, reprinted in *The Permanence of Yeats*, James Hall and Martin
Steinmann, eds. Less readable, but highly impressive, are Cur-
tis Bradford's study of Yeats's interest in Byzantium and of
the manuscripts, in *PMLA* 75 (March 1960), pp. 110-25, reprinted
in *Yeats*, John Unterecker, ed., and Jon Stallworthy's discussion
of the manuscripts in *Between the Lines*. For a hostile discussion of the poem, see Yvor Winters, *Forms of Discovery*. The
capital of the Eastern Roman Empire (330 to 1453) and the "holy
city" of the Greek Orthodox Church, Byzantium's culture is
noted for mysticism, the preservation of ancient learning, and
exquisitely refined symbolic art. In short, its culture (as
Yeats saw it) was wise and passionless. In *A Vision*, his prose
treatment of his complex mystical system, Yeats says:

> I think that in early Byzantium, maybe never before or
> since in recorded history, religious, aesthetic and
> practical life were one, that architect and artificers
> -- though not, it may be, poets, for language has been
> the instrument of controversy and must have grown ab-
> stract -- spoke to the multitude and the few alike.
> The painter, the mosaic worker, the worker in gold and
> silver, the illuminator of sacred books, were almost
> impersonal, almost perhaps without the consciousness
> of individual design, absorbed in their subject matter
> and that the vision of the whole people. They could
> copy out of old Gospel books those pictures that
> seemed as sacred as the text, and yet weave all into
> a vast design, the work of many that seemed the work
> of one, that made building, picture, pattern, metal-
> work of rail and lamp, seem but a single image.

Suggested Topic for Writing:

The pattern of organization in "Sailing to Byzantium."

William Butler Yeats, "Lapis Lazuli." The poem was written in
July 1936; Italy had invaded Abyssinia in 1935, Spain was
torn by civil war, and German preparations for war were evident. The "hysterical women" of the first line reject artists
as "gay" because -- these women believe -- artists are fiddling
while Rome is burning. ("King Billy" probably glances back at
both Kaiser Wilhelm and at King William who in 1690 defeated
the army of King James in Ireland, i.e., back at earlier moments of impending disaster.) "Gay" of course has none of the
modern meaning; in line 3, as used by the "hysterical women,"
it implies irresponsible lightheadedness, but later in the
poem, in line 16 and in the last line, Yeats gives it a pro-
founder meaning, a sense of sublime or heroic joy achieved in
the face of destruction.

After the first stanza the poem is a defense of the arts that
the hysterical women reject. The tragic heroes experience an
illumination that blacks out all ordinary activities (lines
16-20). The artist is not crushed by defeat, but transforms
defeat into triumph. (Yeats was fond of quoting Lady Gregory's
assertion that "Tragedy must be a joy to the man who dies.")
The third stanza records the destruction of successive civili-
zations, including the destruction of works of art, but the
creators nevertheless are "gay." In the fifth stanza Yeats
describes a work of art (the carved stone) that has been dis-
colored and cracked by time but that has turned the work of
time (at least in the eyes of the beholder) to its own ends,
for "Every accidental crack or dent, / Seems a water-course
or an avalanche." The poet imagines that the carved figures
share his view of the carved landscape, for their eyes are not
mournful but "gay." Most of the poem, then, is an assertion
that the arts (tragedy, sculpture, music) are ecstatic rather
than, as asserted at the beginning, trivial.

If you teach this poem in connection with *Hamlet*, you may also
want to use a quotation from Yeats's *On the Boiler*, reprinted
in his *Explorations* (Macmillan, 1962), pp. 448-49:

> The arts are all the bridal chambers of joy. No
> tragedy is legitimate unless it leads some great
> character to his final joy. Polonius may go out
> wretchedly, but I can hear the dance music in
> "Absent thee from felicity awhile," or in Hamlet's
> speech over the dead Ophelia. . . . I add that
> "will or energy is eternal delight," and when its
> limit is reached it may become a pure, aimless joy,
> though the man, the shade, still mourns his lost
> object.

Edward Arlington Robinson, "Richard Cory." The point is not
that money doesn't bring happiness; even a thoroughly civilized
spirit (grace, taste, courtesy) does not bring happiness. The
protagonist's name is significant. "Richard" suggests "rich,"
and probably his entire name faintly suggests Richard Coeur de
Lion (and *coeur* = heart and core, and also suggests *cour* =
court). These suggestions, along with "crown," "favored,"
"imperially" "arrayed," "glittered," "king," emphasize his
wealth and power, but other words in the poem emphasize his
dignity, courtesy, and humanity: "gentleman," "clean favored,"
"quietly," "human," "schooled," "grace." Everything combines
to depict him as a man of self-sufficiency, dignity, and restraint -- yet he kills himself. Still, even his final act
has some dignity: it is stated briefly, and it takes place on
"one calm summer night." Students might be asked if anything
is lost by substituting (what might on first thought seem more
appropriate) "one dark winter night." If this rewriting is
not bad enough, listen to Paul Simon's version of the poem.
He sings it, with Art Garfunkel, on *Sounds of Silence*, Columbia recording CS 9269.

Edward Arlington Robinson, "Mr. Flood's Party." Cleanth Brooks,
R. W. B. Lewis, and R. P. Warren, in *American Literature*, vol.
II, p. 1844, point out that among Robinson's poems, "Mr. Flood's
Party" is fairly unusual in its shifts of tone. There is the
language of the poet, making, for example, a reference to the
medieval epic, *The Song of Roland* (or possibly to Browning's
"Childe Roland"), and there is the contrasting language of Mr.
Flood speaking to himself: "Well, Mr. Flood, / Since you pro-
pose it, I believe I will." But of course the effect of the
reference to Roland is both to diminish Mr. Flood, by almost
comically comparing this tippling old man with a heroic war-
rior, and also to elevate him by reminding us of the heroism
of the lonely man. Notice too that Mr. Flood himself uses the
"poetic diction" of "the bird is on the wing" (quoting from
the *Rubáiyát*), and "auld lang syne." Another point: the poem
is saved from sentimentality (the old man now friendless)
largely by Flood's slightly comic (as well as pathetic) polite-
ness.

Robert Frost, "Design." On Frost's "Design," see Randall
Jarrell, *Poetry and the Age*; Richard Ohmann in *College English*
28 (February 1967), pp. 359-67; *Frost: Centennial Essays*; and
Reginald Cook, *Robert Frost: A Living Voice*, especially pp.
263-67. "Design" was published in 1922; below is an early
(1912) version of the poem.

A dented spider like a snow drop white
On a white Heal-all, holding up a moth
Like a white piece of lifeless satin cloth--
Saw ever curious eye so strange a sight?--
Portent in little, assorted death and blight
Like the ingredients of a witches' broth?--
The beady spider, the flower like a froth,
And the moth carried like a paper kite.

What had that flower to do with being white,
The blue prunella every child's delight.
What brought the kindred spider to that height?
(Make we no thesis of the miller's plight.)
What but design of darkness and of night?
Design, design! Do I use the word aright?

The changes, obvious enough, are discussed by George Monteiro,
in *Frost: Centennial Essays*, Committee on the Frost Centennial
of the University of Southern Mississippi, eds., pp. 335-38.

Robert Frost, "The Wood-Pile." The poem contrasts man, who
"can forget his handiwork" because he lives for "turning to
fresh tasks," with nature, a "frozen swamp" that is "Too much
alike to mark or name a place by"; the swamp is not even a
"here," but only something that tells the speaker he is "far
from home." Nature is nothing in itself -- or rather, nothing
meaningful to man -- until man gives it meaning; in this poem,
meaning is imposed on it by the person who built the woodpile.
And even though the wood is not burning in the fireplace, it
nevertheless has been made into something coherent, and it
shows the mark of man as it rots and "warm[s] the frozen swamp
as best it could." Nature, then, needs man's collaboration,
and, conversely, man needs nature's collaboration, for nature
completes what man has abandoned. On this last point, notice
that "Clematis / Had wound strings round and round it like a
bundle" -- though the line also suggests that nature is re-
claiming from man what is hers. For an excellent discussion
of the poem, see Richard Poirier, *Robert Frost*.

William Carlos Williams, "Spring and All." Williams's "Spring
and All," the first poem in his book (1922) of the same title,
is preceded by eleven pages of prose, the gist of which is the
defense of a "new" American experimental writing. This introduction concludes with the words "THE WORLD IS NEW," and then
the poem bursts upon us. It begins with the reference to the
hospital (stock responses -- which Williams dedicated his life
to opposing -- conjure up ideas of sickness and death, but it

turns out that the poem moves on to the recovery of health,
which after all is what hospitals are for); it moves on to
vivid concrete description of bushes and trees that appear
"Lifeless," then to a spring that "quickens," and finally
back to the bushes and trees that "begin to awaken." What is
"contagious" turns out to be not sickness, death, winter (all
stock responses), but spring, and probably this contagious
quality of spring is what the "All" of the title implies.
Characteristically, Williams seems "unpoetic": although in
line 2 "the surge of clouds" is metaphoric (clouds as waves),
and in line 7 "standing water" is a metaphor (though only a
dead metaphor), one can say that in the first part of the poem
figurative language is conspicuously absent. Not until line
15 ("dazed spring approaches") does figurative language emerge;
the following stanza (lines 16-20) continues the image of
nature as human ("They enter the new world naked"), making it
clear that the hospital is as much a place of birth as of
death, and essentially a place where life is preserved, but
the poem also continues to record sharp literal perceptions
("the stiff curl of wildcarrot leaf"), enhancing the last,
metaphoric words: "rooted they / grip down and begin to
awaken." The slight increase in the number of verbs (they
are sparse in the beginning) helps to suggest the life that
is pushing through the deadness. Whether literal or metaphoric, the lines seek (to borrow words which Williams used
of his *Kora in Hell*) "to refine, to clarify, to intensify that
eternal moment in which we alone live." See also, for a long
discussion, Bram Dijkstra, *Cubism, Stieglitz, and the Earlier
Poetry of William Carlos Williams*.

<u>William Carlos Williams, "A Sort of a Song.</u>" Williams's life-
long concern with scrubbing the debris off words so that they
really mean something is of course evident in "A Sort of a
Song," which can be related to many of his prose statements.
For example, in "How to Write" he says that there must be a
"cracking up of phrases which have stopped the mind," and this
must be done so that we can genuinely experience the present.
(Compare "Spring and All": "One by one objects are defined --
It quickens: clarity, outline of leaf.") Like many of Williams's poems, "A Sort of a Song" is concerned with hidden
forces striking out (again compare "Spring and All," with its
unstated but evident admiration for the vegetation that is
poking through the debris of winter), i.e., a celebration of
the energy of the apparently ordinary, caught at the moment
of birth. Perhaps for students the most difficult part of
"A Sort of a Song" is the beginning of the second stanza:
" -- through metaphor to reconcile / the people and the
stones." The idea is a reconciliation of opposites, for

stones (in contrast to people) are about as inert and lifeless as anything we can imagine; and stones (again in contrast to people) are about as enduring as anything we can imagine.

Marianne Moore, "Poetry." See Lloyd Frankenberg, *Pleasure Dome*, pp. 137-41, and R. P. Blackmur, *Language as Gesture*, pp. 266-68. In an interview in *Paris Review*, reprinted in *Writers at Work, Second Series*, Miss Moore comments on her extensive use of quotations: "I was just trying to be honorable and not to steal things. I've always felt that if a thing has been said in the *best* way, how can you say it better? If I wanted to say something and somebody had said it ideally, then I'd take it but give the person credit for it. That's all there is to it. If you are charmed by an author, I think it's a very strange and invalid imagination that doesn't long to share it. Somebody else should read it, don't you think?" And perhaps the following comment, also in the interview, is relevant: "Do the poet and scientist not work analogously? Both are willing to waste effort. To be hard on himself is one of the main strengths of each. Each is attentive to clues, each must narrow the choice, must strive for precision. . . . The objective is fertile procedure. Is it not?"

T. S. Eliot, "The Love Song of J. Alfred Prufrock" and "Journey of the Magi." Among the useful introductory books are Elizabeth Drew, *T. S. Eliot*; Northrop Frye, *T. S. Eliot*; and Grover Smith, *T. S. Eliot's Poetry and Plays*. On "Prufrock" see also Rosenthal and Smith, *Exploring Poetry*; Hugh Kenner, *The Invisible Poet: T. S. Eliot*, pp. 3-12; and Lyndall Gordon, *Eliot's Early Years*. It is well to alert students to the fact that "Prufrock" is not a Browningesque dramatic monologue with a speaker and a listener but rather an internal monologue in which "I" (the timid self) addresses his own amorous self as "you." (Not every "you" in this poem, however, refers to Prufrock's amorous self. Sometimes "you" is equivalent to "one.") Possibly, too, the "you" is the reader, or even other people who, like Prufrock, are afraid of action.

The first twenty lines of "Journey of the Magi," in which "and" occurs fourteen times, seem to be a matter-of-fact account, almost an entry in a journal. Except for "we regretted" in line 8, the speaker reveals almost nothing of his feelings. That is, we get nothing of the exuberance of the Magi as we know them in Christmas carols, or as the Bible describes them ("They rejoiced with exceeding great joy"). The second part (lines 21-31) resembles the first, but the lines on the whole are longer, the rhythm easier, and the references to the New

Testament (three trees -- suggesting the three crosses on
Golgotha -- white horse, vine, wineskins, dicing for silver)
all help to mark a change in tone, though there is still great
restraint, notably in "(you may say)" in line 31. The speaker
does not report anything that looks much like a picture of the
infant Christ surrounded by adoring shepherds and angels. In
the third (final) section the speaker gives his reactions and
reveals the impact of the experience: he does not know its
meaning, but he senses its importance, and, no longer at ease
in his world, he longs for a death that will liberate him.
The conversion, as the Magus moves from his old life toward
a new one, is not sudden and satisfying, but slow and dis-
turbing. He yearns for "another death" -- his own -- to release him from his spiritual struggle. The poem doubtless
has autobiographical elements. Eliot published it in 1927,
the year that he was confirmed in the Anglican Church. On
"Journey of the Magi" see Kenner, *The Invisible Poet*, pp. 243-
50. Eliot reads "Prufrock" on *T. S. Eliot Reading His Poetry*
(Caedmon Recording, TC 1045).

Suggested Topics for Writing:

1. The role of landscape in "Prufrock" or "Journey."
2. Unifying devices in "Prufrock."
3. The role of allusion in "Prufrock."

Archibald MacLeish, "Ars Poetica." See Donald Stauffer, *The
Nature of Poetry*, pp. 121-25, and V. P. Standt in *College
English* 19 (October 1957), pp. 28-29. Standt points out that
in the first and second sections there are similes, but in the
third section we move from similarity to identity, i.e., metaphors replace similes. Moreover, identity is stressed in the
quasi-mathematical formula at the beginning of the third section. This poem, like Moore's "Poetry," easily gets the class
into a discussion of the nature of art. (Moore's poem is not
concerned explicitly with "modern" poetry but with new poetry
of any period.) And a discussion of MacLeish's poem inevitably
gets into whether MacLeish practices his precepts; the abundant
detail gives us a sense of felt reality ("be"), but doesn't
MacLeish also "mean"? Certainly "a poem should not mean but
be" has meaning; and note, too, that MacLeish is not content
to give us "An empty doorway and a maple leaf," for he prefaces
this with an explanation, telling us that it stands "for all
the history of grief." By the way, if one wishes to pursue
this topic in class, one might link MacLeish's poem with W. C.
Williams's "A Sort of a Song," an imagist poem that proclaims
"No ideas but in things." It is useful to ask students to
comment in detail on the figures. The figure of an empty

90

doorway and an autumn leaf, standing for grief, is clear
enough, but how is "a poem . . . motionless in time / As the
moon climbs"? Perhaps the idea is that a poem, because it
stirs the emotions, seems to move; yet it is itself unchanging.

E. E. Cummings, "anyone lived in a pretty how town." It can
be useful to ask students to put into the usual order (so far
as one can) the words of the first two stanzas, and then to
ask students why Cummings's version is more effective. Here
are a few rough glosses: 1.4: "danced his did" = lived intensely (versus the "someones" who in 1.18 "did their dance,"
i.e., unenthusiastically went through motions that might have
been ecstatic); 1.7: "they sowed their isn't they reaped their
same" gives us the little-minded or small-minded who, unlike
"anyone," are unloving and therefore receive nothing; 1.8:
"sun moon stars rain" = day after day; 1.10: "down they forgot
as up they grew" implies a mental diminution that accompanies
growing up; 1.17: "someones," i.e., adults, people who think
they are somebody; 1.25: "anyone died," i.e., the child ma-
tured, stopped loving (and became dead as the other adults).
The last two stanzas imply that although children grow into
lifeless adults, childhood is not extinguished, for there will
be a new generation ("earth by april," 1.31), and these too
will grow into "Women and men" (1.33) as the seasons continue.
(This reading is heavily indebted to R. C. Walsh, *Explicator*
22, no. 9 [May 1964], Item 72. For a more complicated reading,
see D. L. Clark, *Lyric Resonance*, pp. 187-94.)

W. H. Auden, "Musée des Beaux Arts" and "The Unknown Citizen."
Useful pieces on "Musée" are in *College English* 24 (April
1963), pp. 529-31; *Modern Language Notes* 76 (April 1961), pp.
331-36; and *Art Journal* 32 (Winter 1972-73), pp. 157-62 -- the
last useful chiefly because it includes reproductions of
Breughel's work and reprints other poems relating to his pic-
tures. Breughel's picture of Icarus (in the Brussels Museum
of Fine Arts, hence Auden's title) is much reprinted, for
example, in Timothy Foote, *The World of Breughel*. Auden
glances at some of Breughel's other paintings (the children
skating, in *The Numbering of Bethlehem*, indifferent to
Joseph and Mary who are almost lost in a crowd; the dogs and
the horses in *The Massacre of the Innocents*), and his poem
accurately catches Breughel's sense of nature undisturbed by
what happens to an individual. As Otto Benesch points out
(*The Art of the Renaissance in Northern Europe*, p. 99), in
Icarus Breughel gives us a sense of cosmic landscape.
Ploughman, shepherd, and fisherman go about their business,
unaware of Icarus; the yellow sun sets in the west, and the

sea, coasts, and islands are transfigured with a silvery light. In Ovid's account in *Metamorphoses* 8.183-235, it should be noted, the ploughman, shepherd, and fisherman beheld Icarus with amazement. Students are at first inclined to see Auden's poem as an indictment of indifference; our own view is that Auden gives the daily world its due, especially in such phrases as "doggy life" and "innocent behind," i.e., Auden helps us to see that all of creation cannot and need not suffer along with the heroes. Auden's poem evoked a pleasant reply by Randall Jarrell, "The Old and the New Masters," *Collected Poems* (1969), pp. 332-33. It begins, "About suffering, about adoration, the old masters / Disagree. . . ."

In "The Unknown Citizen" the speaker's voice is obviously not the poet's. The speaker -- appropriately unidentified in a poem about a society without individuals -- apparently is a bureaucrat. For such a person, a "saint" is not one who is committed to spiritual values but one who causes no trouble.

Suggested Topic for Writing:

What is Auden satirizing in "The Unknown Citizen"? Students might be cautioned to spend some time thinking about whether Auden is satirizing the speaker, the citizen, conformism, totalitarianism, technology, or what.

Theodore Roethke, "Elegy for Jane." The speaker compares Jane to a fish (pickerel), to birds (wren, sparrow, pigeon), and to vegetation (fern) -- but he makes the point that "the sides of wet stones cannot console me, / Nor the moss, wound with the last light." His suggestion thus is that although he insistently asserts that she is closely related to nature, resembling a small wild creature, he can get no consolation from his perception of nature (the sight of "wet stones" and "moss"), for he realizes that Jane is *not* really "a wren," "my sparrow," etc. but something of a quite different nature. Roethke commented on the rhythm of this piece in *Poetry* 97 (October 1960), pp. 35-46, reprinted in *Conversations on the Craft of Poetry*, Cleanth Brooks and R. P. Warren, eds., and again in Roethke's *On the Poet and His Craft*, pp. 71-84. Roethke explains that even in free verse there is "the ghost of some other form, often blank verse, behind what is written or the more elaborate rise and fall of the rhythmical prose sentence." He contrasts Ransom's "Bells for John Whiteside's Daughter," a "formal poem," with his own "Elegy for Jane," a "more proselike piece," and calls attention to "the listing, the appositions, and the absolute construction" at the beginning of "Elegy for Jane," the "triad" at the end of the first stanza ("The shade,"

"The leaves," "And the mold"), the successive shortening of
the last three lines of the second and third stanzas, which
contrasts with the successive lengthening of the last three
lines of the first stanza. Harvey Gross, *Sound and Form in
Modern Poetry*, examines Roethke's prosody.

Robert Hayden, "Those Winter Sundays." First, a confession:
we thought about glossing "offices" in the last line, for students will almost surely misinterpret the word, thinking that
it refers to places where white-collar workers do their tasks.
But we couldn't come up with a concise gloss that would convey
the sense of ceremonious and loving performance of benefits.
And it may be just as well to spend some class time on this
important word, because the thing as well as the word may be
unfamiliar to many students. After the word has been discussed, the poem may read as a splendid illustration of it.

One may want to raise the question in class of whether the
knowledge that the author was black affects the poem's meaning.

Dylan Thomas, "Fern Hill." "Fern Hill" is discussed in William York Tindall, *A Reader's Guide to Dylan Thomas; Explicator* 14 (October 1955), Item 1; *Critical Quarterly* 1 (Summer
1959), pp. 134-38; Elizabeth Drew and George Connor, *Dis-
covering Modern Poetry*. Thomas recites the poem on Caedmon
Records 1002. James G. Kennedy in *College English* 31 (March
1970), pp. 585-86, dwelling on the last two lines ("Time held
me green and dying / Though I sang in my chains like the sea"),
argues that the child "may have been stunted by his being let
alone, as if he were a unique being, and by his being furnished
with unrealistic ideas about the world. . . . The last line of
'Fern Hill' is powerful in its evocation of how the mind of
bourgeois man may be fettered for life by a *laissez faire* boyhood." This quotation should provoke lively response.

Randall Jarrell, "The Woman at the Washington Zoo." Jarrell
discusses the poem, especially its progress through several
drafts, in Brooks and Warren, *Understanding Poetry*, 4th ed.,
reprinted in *The Poet's Work*, Reginald Gibbons, ed. We ex-
tract a few comments, but the entire discussion is recommended.
The speaker, a woman employed by the government, despairingly
feels that her faded navy blue print dress is a sort of uniform. She knows that she attracts no attention, and that her
days (like her clothes) are humdrum. She looks into the eyes
of the caged animals and sees a reflection, i.e., sees herself
as caged. The animals, however, are *not* like her. As Jarrell

says in his commentary, the poem begins with "colored women and colored animals and colored cloth -- all that the woman sees as her opposite"; the saris of Indian and Pakistani women in Washington, he explains in the commentary, seem to be "cloth from another planet." "Inside the mechanical official cage of her life, her body," Jarrell explains, "she lives invisibly; no one feeds the animal -- . . . the cage is empty," whereas the caged wild animals retain their identity as wild animals. The natural, wild world ("sparrows," "pigeons," and then, more loathesome, "buzzards") visits the caged wild beasts, but no one of her tribe comes to her. She herself has become dead flesh, like the buzzards' food. "Her own life is so terrible to her that, to change, she is willing to accept even this, changing it as best she can." She hopes that under the ugly bird's red head and black wings is a human being, not a lifeless creature like herself.

Gwendolyn Brooks, "We Real Cool." This poem goes well in discussions of the speaking tone of voice, and also in discussions of rhythm. Notice how the "We" at the end of each line is, because of its position, given a little extra emphasis; one tends to pause (even if almost imperceptibly) after each "we," even though the word is not followed by a comma. There is interesting autobiographical material (letters, interviews, etc.) in Brooks's *Report from Part One*. In it she explains (p. 185) that the "we's" in "We Real Cool" are "weakly argumentative" assertions by "boys [who] have no accented sense of themselves, yet they are aware of a semi-defined personal importance." Brooks reads the poem on *The Spoken Arts Treasury of 100 Modern American Poets*, vol. 13 (SA 1052).

Robert Lowell, "Mr. Edwards and the Spider." Lowell's sources are Edwards's "Of Insects" and "Sinners in the Hands of an Angry God." The first stanza begins with Edwards's sensitive perception of "the spiders marching through the air." The purposiveness of "marching" is nicely joined with a sense of pleasure in "Swimming from tree to tree," but even in these first lines there is an ominous note, for the day is "mildewed," and, since the hay is being brought to the barn, this is a time of harvest, i.e., of death amidst richness. From the fourth line, on to the end of the first stanza, we learn that the spiders are being swept by the wind to the ocean, where they will die. The second stanza makes it clear that we, like the spiders, are subject to a divine will. We, too, one understands, seek our "ease" (line 8), even our "sunrise" (line 9), which seems hopeful, but we go to destruction. Our efforts to protect ourselves with "thorn and briar / In battle

array" are useless against "treason crackling in your blood"
(line 13). The last line of the second stanza sounds pitying,
but the latter part of the third stanza (lines 24-27), and the
entire fourth stanza are stern, even cruel, and surely at
least here and in the fifth stanza we can feel that the poet
invites us to look askance at the Calvinistic speaker who
thinks he is praising God's majesty. For a good discussion
of the poem, see Alan Williamson, *Pity the Monsters: The
Poetical Vision of Robert Lowell.* See also Dallas E. Wiebe in
Wisconsin Studies in Contemporary Literature 3, No. 2 (Spring-
Summer 1962), pp. 22-27.

Lawrence Ferlinghetti, "Constantly risking absurdity." Ferlinghetti has insisted that poetry be read aloud, and as a
consequence he writes poetry that is easily intelligible to
auditors. (Not surprisingly, the one allusion in Ferlinghetti's
poem is not to mythology or literature but to the liveliest and
most popular art, film.) Easy intelligibility, however, means
that the poet is "constantly risking absurdity." Of course
the point is not to be absurd; absurdity is a risk one runs in
trying to "perceive / taut truth" as one approaches "Beauty"
and hopes to catch her. The shape of the poem on the page more
or less imitates the progress and the pauses of a performer on
a tightrope, and perhaps it also imitates his balancing pole
extending far out on each side. The poem is obviously related
to many of William Carlos Williams's poems, especially to "The
Artist." And it is worthwhile reminding students of Frost's
comment that a poem is a "performance in words." In addition
to Ferlinghetti's typographical performance on paper, the wordplay is part of the act ("climbs on rime," "balancing on eye-
beams," "sleight-of-foot tricks," "with gravity").

May Swenson, "A Navajo Blanket." The poem has fourteen lines
and thus can be considered a sonnet, though it is unrhymed and
written not as an octave and sestet or as three quatrains and
a couplet, but as two units of seven lines each. The first
part of the first unit emphasizes the energy of the brightly
colored blankets of a type called Eye-Dazzlers: "Eye-dazzlers,"
"pull," "pin you," "Brightness," all are appropriate initial
responses to these vigorous, even aggressive, blankets of
bright colors and (usually) bold diamonds, chevrons, and
stripes. But in the fourth line, "Alight" introduces the
motif of resting, and it is clarified by the comparison to a
"calm and hooded" hawk. The hawk is said "to fasten to the
forearm of a Chief," but in the second unit (beginning with
line 7) we move further downward or inward and are wrapped, as
the Indian is, within the blanket. (These blankets were worn

as a cape, over one or both shoulders, and pulled forward by
the arms within. They were also used as mats to sit on, or as
beds.) Swenson apparently assumes -- against the views of
most specialists -- that the pattern of the blankets is symbolic, with a comforting Sun and Moon and a representation of
the "spirit trail" (a name given to Navajo rituals celebrating
any rite of passage, such as puberty, marriage, pregnancy, departure for war). In any case, the blanket first dazzles, then
calms and nourishes, then releases and purifies and restores,
its vibrant colors paradoxically giving the mind the simplicity
of "a white cup."

Why are the names of the colors capitalized? Perhaps to emphasize their mystical or symbolic nature. Why are the initial
words of each line not capitalized? Perhaps to emphasize the
continuity, the steady pull that the blanket exerts as it draws
one in.

Anthony Hecht, "The Dover Bitch." The subtitle ("A Criticism
of Life") as well as the title, is derived from Arnold, who in
"The Study of Poetry," *Essays in Criticism, Second Series*,
speaks of poetry as "a criticism of life." Hecht's poem is
also a criticism of poetry (though Arnold's "Dover Beach" --
printed in *An Introduction to Literature* -- survives it).
Arnold's allusion to Sophocles, mentioned in "Dover Bitch"
(lines 7-8), apparently is to *Antigone*, line 469; at least no
more relevant passage exists in Sophocles. Inevitably Hecht's
poem must be discussed in connection with Arnold's, but sooner
or later the discussion probably ought to get to matters of
tone in "Dover Bitch." (Andrews Wanning, to whom the poem is
dedicated, is a teacher of literature.)

Allen Ginsberg, "A Supermarket in California." The poem evokes
Walt Whitman by name, and evokes his poetry in the long, unrhymed lines and in the catalogs of commonplace objects of
American life. But Ginsberg's America is not Whitman's, for
Ginsberg seeks "the lost America of love" -- though Ginsberg
makes the point that Whitman too was lonely while he lived
and finally encountered the loneliness of death. The allusion
to the Spanish poet Garcia Lorca is to his poem on Walt Whitman, and also calls to mind yet another homosexual poet whose
love was unreciprocated.

Donald Hall, "Names of Horses." These horses labor in all the
seasons, seven days a week (for them Sunday is just a day for
a slightly different sort of work), and when they can no

longer work they are shot. But there is no suggestion that
their owners are cruel or even indifferent; indeed, in line
23, when goldenrod is set above the horse's grave, there is a
suggestion of a loving tribute. Lines 25-27 suggest that the
horses have almost become one with nature, but only "almost,"
for the agitation implied in "pushed" is amplified in line 28,
when the frost heaves their bones. There is, even in death,
apparently no rest for the weary. The catalogue or invocation of names of dead horses in the last line, by the way,
ends appropriately with a horse named "Lady Ghost," for these
horses haunt the mind of the poet.

Adrienne Rich, "Living in Sin." If some of the woman's perceptions seem to indicate hyperesthesia (she hears "each separate
stair . . . writhe"), for the most part her perceptions are
fairly ordinary: "last night's cheese," bugs among the saucers,
and so on. The man, however, does not perceive even these,
and for the moment -- since we see him through her eyes -- he
seems utterly oafish. Later she is back in love -- more concerned with the man than with the things around them -- but
this is not a love poem, and the real interest is in the woman's diminished (more reasonable) view of love, even though
she is now back in love. If the stairs no longer "writhe,"
she is nevertheless conscious of them and of the "relentless
day." Presumably never again will she think the studio will
"keep itself"; now she knows that love is not the whole of
life.

Gary Snyder, "Hay for the Horses." This poem (like all good
poems, when you think about it) lets us hear an interesting
voice, or, rather, two voices: the speaker of the first sixteen lines does not explicitly offer his opinion of the man
who "had driven half the night," but we sense his respect; the
old man who speaks lines 19-24 seems to regard his life as
wasted but we hear no self-pity, and whatever hint of bitter-
ness may be in the lives is suffused with an engaging sense of
irony.

Sylvia Plath, "Daddy." C. B. Cox and A. R. Jones point out,
in *Critical Quarterly* 6 (Summer 1964), pp. 107-22, that literature has always been interested in perverse states of mind
(cf. Greek and Roman interest in the irrational; Elizabethan
interest in melancholy, jealousy, madness, etc.; and Browning's
dramatic monologues). The "fine frenzy" of the poet himself
(in the words of Shakespeare's Theseus), once associated with
inspiration and even divinity, in the twentieth century links

the poet with the psychotic personality. And apparently a
sensitive (poetic) mind can make only a deranged response in
a deranged world. Miss Plath's "Daddy" begins with simple
repetitions that evoke the world of the nursery rhyme (and yet
also of the witches in *Macbeth*, who say, "I'll do, I'll do,
and I'll do"). The opening line also connects with the suggestion of the marriage service ("And I said I do") in line
67. The speaker sees herself as tormented yet also as de-
siring the pain inflicted by her father / lover ("Every woman
adores a Fascist"). She recognizes that by accepting the need
for love she exposes herself to violence. The speaker's iden-
tification of herself with Jews, and the evocation of "Dachau,
Auschwitz, Belsen," suggests some identity between the heroine's
tortured mind and the age's. Death, Cox and Jones go on to say,
is the only release from a world that denies love and life.
The "daddy" of the poem is father, German fatherland, and --
most inclusively -- life itself, which surrounds the speaker
and which the speaker rejects. In *Commentary* (July 1974 and
October 1974), there is an exchange of letters on the appropriateness of Plath's use of Nazi imagery in a poem about her
father. Roger Hoffman, in the July issue, argues that the
imagery is valid because in a child's mind an authoritarian
father is fearsome. Irving Howe, in October, pp. 9-12, replies that this argument is inadequate ground "for invoking the
father as a Nazi." The speaker of the poem is not a child,
Howe says, but "the grown-up writer, Sylvia Plath." He goes
on: "the unwarranted fusion of child's response and grown-ups'
references makes for either melodrama or self-pity." Howe also
rejects Carole Stone's argument (July) that the images are
acceptable because "one individual's psyche [can] approximate
the suffering of a people." Howe replies that the victims of
the concentration camps didn't merely "suffer"; they were me-
thodically destroyed. He questions the appropriateness of
using images of the camps to evoke personal traumas. There is,
he says, a lack of "congruence" between the object and the
image, "a failure in judgment." Some useful criticism can
also be found in *The Art of Sylvia Plath*, Charles Newman, ed.

Dona Stein, "Putting Mother By." The title is taken from the
common expression used in canning or otherwise preserving food:
"putting food by." Ms. Stein writes that she "wrote the poem
soon after [she] discovered a recipe for half-sour pickles and
made lots of them," hence the spices in the poem. She also
mentions that although the speaker says of herself and her
siblings, "We are too tiny," it is "the powerful mother who
is small and helpless. We get to carry out what we truly
want -- to keep a parent forever as we recall her in childhood -- unaged, permanently the dreaded and beloved power of

our lives. This is the triumph suggested in fairy-tale justice."

Lucille Clifton, "In the Inner City." This poem -- from a
book called *Good Times* -- catches a distinctive voice, medi-
tative and colloquial, the colloquialisms never slipping into
merely cute dialect or local color.

Seamus Heaney, "The Skunk." If metaphysical poetry is a yoking
of opposites, this is a metaphysical poem, for the poet compares and more or less identifies a skunk -- a beast normally
regarded with some aversion -- with his beloved wife. The
first stanza celebrates the elegance of the skunk, and the
second suggests that its arrival is solemn and momentous. But
note, too, that in "voyeur" the speaker introduces an element
of sexual interest. The next two stanzas are devoted to the
wife who, though absent, seems omnipresent. The fifth stanza
abruptly returns to the skunk, though "she" in the first line
of this stanza (line 17) links the stanza to the woman also.
In the final stanza, "sootfall," with its suggestion of black-
ness falling as silently as soot, refers chiefly to the woman
dropping her black clothing when she undresses at night, but
it also suggests the silent appearance of the skunk. And in
the last two lines the wife is humorously seen as resembling
a skunk, "head-down, tail-up," looking for a black nightdress.

Don L. Lee, "But He Was Cool." Lee's poetry, like some of the
poetry of Imamu Amiri Baraka (LeRoi Jones), owes something to
William Carlos Williams and to Williams's descendants, the
beat poets, though of course the beats were indebted to the
rhythms of jazz, and so ultimately the chief sources are black
speech and black music. The influence of black speech is apparent in a quality that Stephen Henderson (*Understanding the
New Black Poetry*, pp. 33-34) calls "virtuoso naming and enu-
merating," a "technique [that] overwhelms the listener," which
may be derived from "the folk practice of fiddling and similar
kinds of wordplay." There is also a fondness for hyperbole,
combined with witty, elegant coolness.

Dave Smith, "The Spring Poem." Dave Smith has kindly furnished
us with this comment on his poem:

> I think if I had to sum up what I think of this poem
> I would use the word "inexorable." To me the poem is
> about forces in opposition, tension, balance. Having

heard the poet Louise Glück say that everyone should write a Spring poem, or a poem about Spring, I thought that both true and reasonable -- except a part of me kept resisting, a kind of small chaotic voice kept saying *no* to the voice of reason. So I thought of an old junk car, the vines that crawl over it in spring, the things that people do in such cars in spring, the way some things are holding on and some are falling apart always -- and no matter what is happening everything goes on singing in its way. In poems this inexorable singing is what lies at the heart of the form/content dichotomy. In "The Spring Poem" it is what accounts for all the possible meanings of *spring* that the poem seeks to include.

In class, or as a writing assignment, one may want to compare this poem with one of the following: Shakespeare's "When daisies pied and violets blue," Hopkins's "Spring," and Williams's "Spring and All."

<u>Nikki Giovanni, "Master Charge Blues.</u>" For some comments on blues, see the note on Langston Hughes's "Evenin' Air Blues," in this manual, p. 45.

NOTE: Many poems of the last few decades have been recorded by their authors. Caedmon Records (505 Eighth Avenue, New York, New York 10018) and Spoken Arts, Inc. (New Rochelle, New York 10801) offer catalogs that enable the instructor to locate them easily.

17

SOME ELEMENTS OF DRAMA

Among useful basic studies are: S. Barnet *et al.*, eds., *Types of Drama* (an anthology with introductions and critical essays); Cleanth Brooks and Robert Heilman, eds., *Understanding Drama* (an anthology with a good deal of critical commentary); J. L. Styan, *The Elements of Drama*; and Eric Bentley, *The Life of the Drama*.

Quem Quaeritis is included merely to show in little the nature of drama, and the instructor will probably not wish to spend much class time on medieval drama. The standard authorities are E. K. Chambers, referred to in *An Introduction to Literature*, and Hardin Craig, *English Religious Drama*; for very brief accounts of medieval drama, see Thomas Marc Parrott and R. H. Ball, *A Short View of Elizabethan Drama*, and A. P. Rossiter, *English Drama*.

<u>John Millington Synge, *Riders to the Sea*</u>. Adequate discussions of *Riders to the Sea* are in Donna L. Gerstenberger's *John Millington Synge* and (on the mythic implications) Robin Skelton's *The Writings of J. M. Synge*. Relevant biographical details, mostly quoted from Synge's *The Aran Islands*, are in David Greene and Edward M. Stephens, *J. M. Synge*. David R. Clark has edited a casebook on *Riders to the Sea*. Raymond Williams, in *Drama from Ibsen to Eliot*, makes this puzzling comment: "The language is an imposed constituent of flavor rather than the essence of the tragedy, and its discovery." Williams also says that the play is pathetic rather than tragic (but so, too, is a great deal of Greek tragedy). It may be best not to get into the problem of the pathetic versus the tragic here; that can wait until the class discussion of *Antigonê*, *The Glass Menagerie*, or *Death of a Salesman*. If, however, one wants to discuss the play in class, some use may be made of Malcolm Pittock's complaint, in *English Studies* 49 (1968), pp. 445-49, that "It is one thing . . . for Maurya to see a vision and believe that vision fulfilled, but quite another for a modern audience, formed in a different cultural background, to believe in such superstition with any real seriousness."

The title comes from Exodus 15:1: "Then sang Moses and the children of Israel this song unto the Lord, . . . I will sing unto the Lord, for he hath triumphed gloriously; the horse and his rider hath he thrown into the sea."

If in your teaching of a tragedy you discuss the character of
the tragic hero and the emotional effect of tragedy, you may
want to introduce Yeats's "Lapis Lazuli" (in our text; discussed in this manual on p. 85).

On tragedy, consult T. R. Henn, *The Harvest of Tragedy*; F. L.
Lucas, *Tragedy* (especially good on "recognition" and "re-
versal"); Oscar Mandel, *A Definition of Tragedy*; Herbert J.
Muller, *The Spirit of Tragedy*; Richard B. Sewall, *The Vision
of Tragedy*; *Tragedy: Modern Essays in Criticism*, Richard B.
Sewall and Laurence Michel, eds.; and George Steiner, *The
Death of Tragedy*.

Sophocles, *Antigonê*. On *Antigonê*, consult two books by H. D.
F. Kitto, *Greek Tragedy*, and especially *Form and Meaning in
Drama*. See also D. W. Lucas, *The Greek Tragic Poets*, and
Cedric H. Whitman, *Sophocles*. Hegel's view, most often known
through Bradley's essay on Hegel in Bradley's *Oxford Lectures*
(and reprinted in *Hegel on Tragedy*, Anne and Henry Paolucci,
eds.), claims that both sides are right and that both are also
wrong because they assert they are exclusively right. (For a
long anti-Hegelian reading, see Brian Vickers, *Towards Greek
Tragedy*, which insists that Creon is brutal and Antigonê is
thoroughly admirable.) Bradley says, "In this catastrophe
neither the right of the family nor that of the state is denied; what is denied is the absoluteness of the claim of
each." Most subsequent commentators take sides, and either
see Creon as a tragic hero (a headstrong girl forces him to
act, and action proves ruinous, not only to her but to him)
or see Antigonê as a tragic heroine (a girl does what she must,
and is destroyed for doing it). The critical conflict shows
no sign of terminating. Mostly we get assertions, such as
D. W. Lucas's "There is no doubt that in the eyes of Sophocles
Creon is wrong and Antigone right," and Cedric Whitman's "Antigone's famous stubbornness, . . . the fault for which she
has been so roundly reproved, is really moral fortitude."

One of the most perceptive remarks on *Antigonê* is by William Arrowsmith, in *Tulane Drama Review* 3 (March 1959), p. 135, where he says that Antigonê, "trying to uphold a principle beyond her own, or human, power to uphold, gradually empties that principle in action, and then, cut off from her humanity by her dreadful heroism, rediscovers herself and love in the loneliness of her death." He suggests, too, that the play insists on "not the opposition between Antigone and Creon, but [on] the family resemblance which joins them in a common doom."

John Ferguson, in *A Companion to Greek Tragedy*, offers a fairly brief, commonsensical, scene-by-scene commentary on the play. Toward the end he argues that Hegel was utterly wrong in his view that both Creon and Antigonê are right. Ferguson points out that Creon "behaves as a tyrant" and that Creon's law "is disastrous for the state." And Antigonê is "wrong," Ferguson says, because although her "view of the situation is the true one," as a woman it was her duty to obey Creon. The play is about Antigonê's *hybris*, and therefore it is properly titled.

Suggested Topics for Writing:

1. Almost all of the questions given after the text of *Antigonê* make good theme topics. On question 7, George E. Dimock, Jr., argues in *Yale Review* 63 (June 1974), p. 577, that the passage in question is "Antigone's rationalization of an action she is no longer whole-hearted about." Dimock believes that "Antigone repents what she has done." But Brian Vickers, in his long discussion of the play in *Towards Greek Tragedy*, gives reasons for insisting that the lines "are to be taken seriously, at face value" (p. 543).
2. What stage business would you invent for Creon or Antigonê at three points in the play?
3. Haimon's role in *Antigonê*.

Among useful books on comedy are: Louis Kronenberger, *The Thread of Laughter*; L. J. Potts, *Comedy*; Morton Gurewitch, *Comedy*; and D. H. Munro, *Argument of Laughter* (on theories of the comic). Two interesting anthologies of essays on comedy are: *Comedy*, Robert W. Corrigan, ed., and *Theories of Comedy*, Paul Lauter, ed.

Molière, *The Misanthrope*. Martin Turnell, in *The Classical Moment*, has a provocative discussion of *The Misanthrope*; several relevant discussions are also in *Molière*, Jacques Guicharnaud, ed. See also Walter Kerr, *Tragedy and Comedy*, pp. 255-62. For an interesting discussion of how Molière tailored the roles in the play to suit the talents of his actors, see Roger W. Herzel, "'Much Depends on Acting': The Original Cast of *Le Misanthrope*," *PMLA* 95 (May 1980), 348-66.

(The following discussion is an abridgement of an afterword in our *Types of Drama: Plays and Essays*, 3rd edition.)

The passion for honesty that drives Molière's misanthrope, Alceste, is said by the equable Éliante to have "its noble, heroic side," and her view has found wide acceptance among audiences and readers. Alceste is sometimes seen as a tragic figure caught in a comic world, and the play is sometimes said to be a sort of tragic comedy. Alceste demands honesty, and he fulminates against flattery and other forms of insincerity that apparently compose the entire life of the other figures. Surrounded by trimmers and gossips and worse, he alone (if we except the gentle Éliante) seems to hold to a noble ideal. The only other ideal given much prominence is Philinte's, a code of such easy tolerance that it is at times almost indistinguishable from mere passive acceptance of everything.

What case can be made that Alceste is comic, not tragic? A few points suggest themselves. First, this champion of honesty is in love (or thinks he is) with a coquette. What can be more comic than the apostle of plain-dealing being himself in the power of the irrational, especially when this power deposits him at the feet of Célimène, a woman who employs all the devices that in others infuriate him? Second, his demand for honesty is indiscriminate; he is as offended at trivial courtesies as at the law's injustice. Philinte "ought to die of self-disgust" for his "crime" of effusively greeting a casual acquaintance whose name he cannot even recall. So disproportionate is Alceste's passion that when he pops onstage in IV.ii, saying to Éliante, "Avenge me, Madame," he is funny, though the words in themselves are scarcely amusing. In the first scene his tirade against Philinte's "loving demonstrations" offered to one who is almost a stranger evokes Philinte's good-natured

> It hardly seems a hanging matter to me;
> I hope that you will take it graciously
> If I extend myself a slight reprieve,
> And live a little longer, by your leave; '

but this droll reply acerbates Alceste:

> How dare you joke about a crime so grave?

Alceste is thus laughably introduced; his passion is comic because it is disproportionate -- and also because it leads to no action.

Alceste's remark about joking provides a thread that may be followed usefully. He cannot take a joke. Whenever he is laughed at, he becomes indignant, but indignation (when motivated by a desire to protect the self from criticism) itself evokes further laughter because of the gap between the indignant man's presentation of himself and his real worth. Comedy does not allow people to strike attitudes. The man who protests that his argument *is* valid, dammit, or that he *has* a sense of humor, or that his opponent is a fool, is likely to evoke laughter by his monolithic insistence on his merit. When Philinte laughs at the old poem Alceste quotes, Alceste resorts to bitter irony, and when told that his frankness has made him ridiculous, he irritably replies:

> So much the better; just what I wish to hear.
> No news could be more grateful to my ear.
> All men are so detestable in my eyes.
> I should be sorry if they thought me otherwise.

He hopes that he will lose his lawsuit, just to prove that the world *is* as bad as he thinks it is. And when Alceste is told

that his hope that he will lose his lawsuit would reduce all
hearers to laughter and would make his name a jest, he ill-
humoredly replies, "So much the worse for jesters." When his
persistent refusal to praise a trivial poem moves two auditors
to laughter, he again employs frigid irony, and concludes the
scene ominously:

> By heaven, Sirs, I really didn't know
> That I was being humorous.
> *Célimène.*   Go, Sir; go;
> Settle your business.
> *Alceste.*   I shall, and when I'm through,
> I shall return to settle things with you.

Alceste, unable to laugh at the folly of others, cannot, of
course, tolerate laughter at himself. When Philinte puts into
practice the frankness Alceste stormily advocates, Alceste's
response is the indignation we have been commenting on. A
sense of humor (as distinct from derisive laughter) involves
the ability to laugh at what one values, and among the things
one values is the self. Children can laugh at surprises and
at the distress of other children, but they cannot laugh at
themselves because they cannot see themselves in perspective,
at a distance, as it were. The mature man can laugh at mimicry
of himself, but the child or the immature adult will, like
Alceste, sulk or fly into a rage.

In *The Misanthrope* it is entirely possible that Molière is in
some degree mimicking himself. In 1662 Molière at forty married Armande Béjart, a woman less than half his age. The marriage seems to have been unhappy, apparently because his wife
enjoyed attracting the attentions of other men. Some critics,
pressing this point, assume that if the play is autobiographical, Alceste must be expressing Molière's point of view, and
therefore he cannot be a comic figure. If anything, the auto-
biographic origin shows only that Molière had (which no one
has doubted) a sense of humor. He could laugh at himself.
Alceste's courtship of Célimène may in some degree represent
Molière's unhappy marriage to a flirtatious and unappreciative
woman, but the point is that Molière apparently could stand
back and laugh at his own exasperation, which Alceste cannot
do. (Molière subtitled the play "The Atrabilious Man in Love";
one cannot hear Alceste speaking thus of himself.) Alceste can
only, rather childishly, try to maintain his way, and demand
that his special merit be noted and rewarded.

> However high the praise, there's nothing worse
> Than sharing honors with the universe.
> Esteem is founded on comparison:

To honor all men is to honor none.
Since you embrace this indiscriminate vice,
Your friendship comes at far too cheap a price;
I spurn the easy tribute of a heart
Which will not set the worthy man apart:
I choose, Sir, to be chosen; and in fine,
The friend of mankind is no friend of mine.

Once or twice, when he confesses that his love for Célimène is irrational, he seems to have some perspective, but mostly the scenes of Alceste as lover serve to reveal again and again his consuming egotism. His love is so great, he tells Célimène, that he wishes she were in some peril so that he could prove his love by saving her. Célimène aptly replies that Alceste's is "a strange benevolence indeed." (By the way, one might ask students to compare this speech of Alceste's with a somewhat similar speech of Torvald's in Act III of *A Doll's House* when he says to Nora, "Often I wish some terrible danger might threaten you, so that I could offer my life and my blood, everything, for your sake.")

The argument thus far has tried to make the point that Alceste is funny -- funny because (among other things) his anger is indiscriminate and disproportionate, because he is a sort of philosopher and yet is in love, and because his *idée fixe*, frankness, when turned against him, exasperates him. But when we return to Éliante's reference to his "noble, heroic side," and we recall his passion for honesty and his passionate desire to be himself, and when we see the hollowness all about him, the comic figure begins to take on a tragic aspect; and when at the end he departs from the stage unrepentant and bitter, banishing himself from the company of men, we feel that the usual comic plot too has taken on a tragic aspect. But this is hardly to say that Alceste is tragic and *The Misanthrope* a tragedy. One cannot, for example, imagine Alceste committing suicide. He is not an Othello.

Finally, it is appropriate to quote a somewhat different view of Alceste. Kenneth Tynan (*Tynan Right and Left*, p. 117) suggests that "Alceste is comic outside and tragic inside. Nearly everything he does is silly; nearly everything he feels is immensely serious, with implications that go far beyond the plight of a particular man rebelling against the hypocrisy of a particular epoch. . . . The play is a comedy of principle; and its hero raises a question that returns every day to pester the conscience. How far should one accept the rules of the society in which one lives? To put it another way: at what point does conformity become corruption?"

20

PLAYS FOR FURTHER STUDY

Sophocles, _Oedipus Rex_. Though interpretations are innumerable, most fall into the following categories:

1. The gods are just; Oedipus is at fault. The gods are innocent because foreknowledge is not foreordaining. (Jesus predicted that Peter would thrice deny him, but this prediction does not mean that Jesus destined Peter to deny him.) The prophecy told what Oedipus would do, but Oedipus did it because of what he was, not because the gods ordained him to do it. As we watch the play, we see a man acting freely -- pursuing a course that leads to the revelation of who he is. (See especially Bernard Knox, _Oedipus at Thebes_, pp. 33-41.) Though Oedipus is often praised for relentlessly pursuing a truth that may destroy him, the fact is that -- until very late in the play -- he believes he is searching for someone other than himself, and, moreover, in this search he too easily assumes that other people are subversive. Oedipus is rash and even cruel in his dealings with Teiresias, Creon, and the shepherd. His rashness is his _hamartia_ and the gods punish him for it. Given the prophecy that was given to Oedipus, a man less rash would have made it his business never to have killed anyone, and never to have married. [But he thought Polybus and Merope were his parents and he knew that the old man (Laios) was not Polybus and that the Queen in Thebes (Jocasta) was not Merope.]

2. The gods are at fault; Oedipus is innocent. When Oedipus asked the oracle who his parents were, the god answered in such a way as to cause Oedipus to leave a place of safety and to go to a tragic destination. Oedipus is a puppet of the gods; his _hamartia_ is not rashness (a moral fault) but simply a mistake: he _un_intentionally killed his father and married his mother. The oracle was not conditional (it did not say "If you do such and such, then such and such will happen"). The play is a tragedy of destiny; notice that at the end of the play no one justifies the gods, i.e., no one exonerates them from forcing evil on Oedipus.

3. Oedipus is on the whole admirable (he pities his suffering kingdom; he has a keen desire to know the truth), but he is not perfect. The matter of his *intention* is irrelevant because the deeds of patricide and incest (irrespective of motive) contain pollution. The gods are mysterious, and though they sometimes shape men's lives terribly they are not evil because they cannot be judged by human standards of justice or morality.

4. Sophocles is not concerned with justice; the play is an exciting story about a man finding out something, and about the greatness of man and about man's limitations.

Walter Kaufmann, *Tragedy and Philosophy*, has a long discussion of *Oedipus Rex*, in the course of which he finds five themes:

1. The play is about man's radical insecurity (epitomized in Oedipus's fall); Oedipus was the first of men, but he fell.

2. The play is about human blindness. Oedipus did not know who he was (i.e., he was ignorant of his parentage); moreover, he was blind to the honesty of Creon and Teiresias.

3. The play is about the curse of honesty. Oedipus's relentless desire to know the truth brings him to suffering. (If one wants to hunt for a tragic "flaw," one can see this trait as a flaw or vice but a more reasonable way of looking at it sees it as a virtue. Would we regard a less solicitous ruler as more virtuous?)

4. The play is about a tragic situation. If Oedipus abandons his quest, he fails his people; if he pursues his quest, he ruins himself.

5. The play is about justice, or, more precisely, about *in*-justice, i.e., about undeserved suffering. (Here we can come back to Kaufmann's third point: the reward of Oedipus's quest for truth is suffering. It is not even clear that he is being justly punished for killing Laius, for Oedipus belongs to the old heroic world, where killing an enemy is celebrated.) Another point about the play as a play about justice: Sophocles talks of *human* justice too. When Oedipus curses the unknown killer of Laius, he does not think that the killer may have acted in self-defense. And Oedipus's desire to punish Creon and Teiresias similarly shows how wide of the mark efforts at human justice may be.

The Norton Critical Edition of *Oedipus Tyrannus*, L. Berkowitz and T. F. Brunner, eds., includes a translation, some relevant passages from Homer, Thucydides, and Euripides, and numerous religious, psychological, and critical studies, including Freud's, whose key suggestion is that the play "moves a modern audience no less than it did the contemporary Greek one" because there is "a voice within us ready to recognize the compelling force of destiny [in the play]. . . . His destiny moves us only because it might have been ours -- because the oracle laid the same curse upon us before our birth as upon him. It is the fate of all of us, perhaps, to direct our first sexual impulse towards our mother and our first hatred and our first murderous wish against our father." An instructor who uses this quotation in class may wish to call attention to the male chauvinism (Freud's "all of us" really means "all males") and may wish to examine the implication that the play is necessarily more moving to males than to females. It may also be relevant to mention that if the Oedipus of the play did have an Oedipus complex, he would have wanted to go to bed with Merope (the "mother" who brought him up) rather than with Jocasta. But perhaps such a view is too literal. Perhaps this is a convenient place to mention that Oedipus's solution of the riddle of the Sphinx (man is the creature who walks on four feet in the morning, two at noon, and three in the evening) is especially applicable to Oedipus himself (the weakest of infants, the strongest of men in his maturity, and desperately in need of a staff in his blind old age), but of course it applies to all of the spectators as well.

In addition to the Norton edition, the following discussions are especially interesting: Stanley Edgar Hyman, *Poetry and Criticism*; H. D. F. Kitto, *Greek Tragedy* and his *Poiesis*; Richmond Lattimore, *The Poetry of Greek Tragedy*; Cedric Whitman, *Sophocles*; Bernard Knox, *Oedipus at Thebes*; Charles Rowan Beye, *Ancient Greek Literature and Society*, especially pp. 306-12; Brian Vickers, *Towards Greek Tragedy*, vol. I.

William Shakespeare, *Hamlet*. Probably the best short study of *Hamlet* is Maynard Mack's "The World of *Hamlet*," *Yale Review* 41 (1952), pp. 502-23, reprinted in the Signet paperback edition of *Hamlet*, in *Tragic Themes*, Cleanth Brooks, ed., and elsewhere. Maurice Charney's *Style in Hamlet* is excellent, and so too is Harley Granville-Barker's book-length essay in *Prefaces to Shakespeare*. The nature of the Ghost has produced a good deal of commentary, most of it summarized in Eleanor Prosser, *Hamlet and Revenge*. She says that for the Elizabethans a ghost can only be one of three things: a soul of a pagan (impossible in this play, for the context is Christian); a soul from Roman Catholic purgatory (impossible in this play, because it seeks revenge); or a devil (which is what Prosser says this Ghost is). Prosser argues that the Ghost is evil because it counsels revenge, it disappears at the invocation of heaven, and it disappears when the cock crows. But perhaps it can be replied that although the Ghost indeed acts suspiciously, this is to build up suspense and to contribute to the play's meaning, which involves uncertainty and the difficulty of sure action. Prosser sees Hamlet as a rebellious youth who deliberately mistreats Ophelia and descends deep into evil (e.g., he spares Claudius at prayers only in order to damn him), but when he returns from England he is no longer the "barbaric young revenger . . . but a mature man of poise and serenity" (p. 217). He is generous to the Grave-diggers and Laertes, "delightful" with Osric. In short, the young rebel has been chastened by experience and by the vision of death, and so he is saved. He "has fought his way out of Hell" (p. 237). Prosser offers a useful corrective to the romantic idea of the delicate prince, and she offers a great deal of information about the attitude toward ghosts, but one need not accept her conclusion that the Ghost is a devil; her evidence about ghosts is incontrovertible on its own grounds but one may feel that, finally, the play simply doesn't square with Elizabethan popular thought about ghosts.

Suggested Topics for Writing:

Many of the questions printed in the text lend themselves to themes, but here are two more possibilities.

1. Cut 1,000 lines from the play so that it can be performed in a reasonable time, and justify your omissions.
2. The uses of prose in *Hamlet*.

Henrik Ibsen, *A Doll's House*. First, it should be mentioned that the title of the play does *not* mean that Nora is the only doll, for the toy house is not merely Nora's; Torvald, as well as Nora, inhabits this unreal world, for Torvald -- so concerned with appearing proper in the eyes of the world -- can hardly be said to have achieved a mature personality.

A Doll's House (1879) today seems more "relevant" than it has seemed in decades, and yet one can put too much emphasis on its importance as a critique of male chauvinism. Although the old view that Ibsen's best-known plays are "problem plays" about remediable social problems rather than about more universal matters is still occasionally heard, Ibsen himself spoke against it. In 1898, for example, he said, "I . . . must disclaim the honor of having consciously worked for women's rights. I am not even quite sure what women's rights really are. To me it has been a question of human rights" (quoted in Michael Meyer, *Ibsen*, vol. II, p. 297). By now it seems pretty clear that *A Doll's House*, in Robert Martin Adams's words (in *Modern Drama*, A. Caputi, ed.), "represents a woman imbued with the idea of becoming a person, but it proposes nothing categorical about women becoming people; in fact, its real theme has nothing to do with the sexes. It is the irrepressible conflict of two different personalities which have founded themselves on two radically different estimates of reality." Or, as Eric Bentley puts it in *In Search of Theater* (p. 350 in the Vintage edition), "Ibsen pushes his investigation toward a further and even deeper subject [than that of a woman's place in a man's world], the tyranny of one human being over another; in this respect the play would be just as valid were Torvald the wife and Nora the husband."

Michael Meyer's biography, *Ibsen*, is good on the background (Ibsen knew a woman who forged a note to get money to aid her husband, who denounced and abandoned her when he learned of the deed), but surprisingly little has been written on the dramaturgy of the play. Notable exceptions are John Northam, *Ibsen's Dramatic Method*, an essay by Northam printed in *Ibsen*, Rolf Fjelde, ed. (in the *Twentieth-Century Views* series), and Elizabeth Hardwick's chapter on the play in her *Seduction and Betrayal*. Northam calls attention to the symbolic use of properties (e.g., the Christmas tree in Act I is in the center of the room, but in Act II, when Nora's world has begun to crumble, it is in a corner, bedraggled, and with burnt-out candles), costume (e.g., Nora's Italian costume is suggestive of pretense; and the black shawl, symbolic of death, becomes, when worn at the end with ordinary clothes, an indication of her melancholy lonely life), gestures (e.g., blowing out the candles, suggesting defeat; the wild dance; the final slamming of the door).

Dorothea Krook, *Elements of Tragedy*, treats the play as a tragedy. She sets forth what she takes to be the four universal elements of the genre (the act of shame or horror, consequent intense suffering, then an increase in knowledge, and finally a reaffirmation of the value of life) and suggests that these appear in *A Doll's House* -- the shameful condition being "the marriage relationship which creates Nora's 'doll's house' situation." Krook calls attention, too, to the "tragic irony" of Torvald's comments on Krogstad's immorality (he claims it poisons a household), and to Nora's terror, which, Krook says, "evokes the authentic Aristotelian pity."

One can even go a little further than Krook goes and make some connections between *A Doll's House* and *Oedipus*. Nora, during her years as a housewife, like Oedipus during his kingship, *thought* that she was happy but finds out that she really wasn't, and at the end of the play she goes out (self-banished), leaving her children, to face an uncertain but surely difficult future. Still, although the play can be discussed as a tragedy, and cannot be reduced to a "problem play," like many of Ibsen's other plays it stimulates a discussion of What ought to be done? and What happened next? Hermann J. Weigand, in *The Modern Ibsen* (1925), offered conjectures about Nora's future actions. He says:

> But personally I am convinced that after putting Torvald through a sufficiently protracted ordeal of suspense, Nora will yield to his entreaties and return home -- on her own terms. She will not bear the separation from her children very long, and her love for Torvald, which is not as dead as she thinks, will reassert itself. For a time the tables will be reversed: a meek and chastened husband will eat out of the hand of his squirrel; and Nora, hoping to make up by a sudden spurt of zeal for twenty-eight years of lost time, will be trying desperately hard to grow up. I doubt, however, whether her volatile enthusiasm will even carry her beyond the stage of resolutions. The charm of novelty worn off, she will tire of the new game very rapidly and revert, imperceptibly, to her role of songbird and charmer, as affording an unlimited range to the exercise of her inborn talents of coquetry and play-acting.

Students may be invited to offer their own conjectures on the unwritten fourth act.

Another topic for class discussion or for an essay, especially relevant to Question 4: Elizabeth Hardwick suggests (*Seduction and Betrayal*, p. 46) that Ibsen failed to place enough emphasis on Nora's abandonment of the children. In putting "the leaving of her children on the same moral and emotional level as the leaving of her husband . . . Ibsen has been too much a man in the end. He has taken the man's practice, if not his stated belief, that where self-realization is concerned children shall not be an impediment." But in a feminist reading of the play, Elaine Hoffman Baruch, in *Yale Review* 69 (Spring 1980), takes issue with Hardwick, and argues that "it is less a desire for freedom than a great sense of inferiority and the desire to find out more about the male world outside the home that drives Nora away from her children" (p. 37).

Finally, one can discuss with students the comic aspects of the play -- the ending (which, in a way, is happy, though of course Nora's future is left in doubt), and especially Torvald's fatuousness. This fatuousness perhaps reaches its comic height early in Act III, when, after lecturing Mrs. Linde on the importance of an impressive exit (he is telling her how, for effect, he made his "capricious little Capri girl" leave the room after her dance), he demonstrates the elegance of the motion of the hands while embroidering, and the ugliness of the motions when knitting. Also comic are his ensuing fantasies, when he tells the exhausted Nora that he fantasizes that she is his "secret" love, though the comedy turns ugly when, after she rejects his amorous advances ("I have desired you all evening"), he turns into a bully: "I'm your husband, aren't I?" The knock on the front door (Rank) reintroduces comedy, for it reduces the importunate husband to conventional affability ("Well! How good of you not to pass by the door."), but of course it also saves Nora from what might have been an ugly assault.

Tennessee Williams, _The Glass Menagerie_. The books on Williams that have appeared so far are disappointing. The best general survey is Henry Popkin's article in _Tulane Drama Review_ 4 (Spring 1960), pp. 45-64; also useful is Gordon Rogoff, in _Tulane Drama Review_ 10 (Summer 1966), pp. 78-92. There is also a brief but good discussion of _The Glass Menagerie_ in Otto Reinert's _Modern Drama_ (Alternate Edition); for a comparison between the play and earlier versions, see Lester A. Beaurline, _Modern Drama_ 8 (1965), pp. 142-49. For a discussion of Christian references and motifs (e.g., Amanda's candelabrum, which was damaged when lightning struck the church), see Roger B. Stein, in _Western Humanities Review_ 18 (Spring 1964) pp. 141-53, reprinted in _Tennessee Williams_, Stephen S. Stanton, ed. Stein suggests that the play shows us a world in which Christianity has been replaced by materialism.

Perhaps the two points that students find most difficult to understand are that Amanda is both tragic _and_ comic (see the comments below, on the first suggested topic for writing), and that Tom's quest for reality has about it something of adolescent romanticism. Tom comes under the influence of his father (who ran away from his responsibilities), and he depends heavily on Hollywood movies. This brings up another point: it is obvious that Amanda, Laura, and Tom cherish illusions, but students sometimes do not see that Williams suggests that all members of society depended in some measure on the illusions afforded by movies, magazine fiction, liquor, dance halls, sex and other things that "flooded the world with brief, deceptive rainbows" while the real world of Berchtesgaden, etc., moving toward World War II, was for a while scarcely seen.

Suggested Topics for Writing:

1. Comedy in *The Glass Menagerie*. (Students should be cautioned that comedy need not be "relief." It can help to modify the tragic aspects, or rather, to define a special kind of tragedy. A few moments spent on the Porter scene in *Macbeth* -- with which almost all students are familiar -- will probably help to make clear the fact that comedy may be integral.)

2. Compare the function of Tom with the function of the Chorus in *Antigonê*. (Williams calls his play a "memory play." What we see is supposed to be the narrator's memory -- not the dramatist's representation -- of what happened. Strictly speaking, the narrator is necessarily unreliable in the scene between Laura and Jim, for he was not present, but as Williams explains in the "Production Notes," what counts is not what happened but what the narrator remembers as having happened, or, more exactly, the narrator's response to happenings.)

3. Symbolic stage properties in *The Glass Menagerie* (the fire escape, the glass animals, the electric lights, the candles).

4. Cinematic techniques in *The Glass Menagerie*. (Among these are: fade-ins and fade-outs; projected titles, reminiscent of titles in silent films; the final "interior pantomime" of Laura and Amanda, enacted while Tom addresses the audience, resembles by its silence a scene from silent films, or a scene in a talking film in which the sound track gives a narrator's voice instead of dramatic dialogue. By the way, it should be noted that Williams, when young, like Tom, often attended movies, and that this play was adapted from Williams's rejected screen play, *The Gentleman Caller*, itself derived from one of Williams's short stories.)
Topics 3 and 4 are ways of getting at the importance of *un*realistic settings and techniques in this "memory play."

5. Compare the play with the earlier Williams short story, "Portrait of a Girl in Glass," in *One Arm and Other Stories*.

Arthur Miller, *Death of a Salesman*. (The discussion of *Death of a Salesman* is an abbreviation of our afterword in *Types of Drama*.) The large question, of course, is whether Willy is a

tragic or a pathetic figure. For the ancient Greeks, at least
for Aristotle, *pathos* was the destructive or painful act common in tragedy; but in English "pathos" refers to an element
in art or life that evokes tenderness or sympathetic pity.
Modern English critical usage distinguishes between tragic
figures and pathetic figures by recognizing some element either
of strength or of regeneration in the former that is not in the
latter. The tragic protagonist perhaps acts so that he brings
his destruction upon himself, or if his destruction comes from
outside, he resists it, and in either case he comes to at
least a partial understanding of the causes of his suffering.
The pathetic figure, however, is largely passive, an unknowing
and unresisting innocent. In such a view Macbeth is tragic,
Duncan pathetic; Lear is tragic, Cordelia pathetic; Othello is
tragic, Desdemona pathetic; Hamlet is tragic (the situation is
not of his making, but he does what he can to alter it), Ophelia pathetic. (Note, by the way, that of the four pathetic
figures named, the first is old and the remaining three are
women. Pathos is more likely to be evoked by persons assumed
to be relatively defenseless than by the able-bodied.)

The guardians of critical terminology, then, have tended to
insist that "tragedy" be reserved for a play showing action
that leads to suffering which in turn leads to knowledge.
They get very annoyed when a newspaper describes as a tragedy
the death of a promising high school football player in an
automobile accident, and they insist that such a death is
pathetic not tragic; it is unexpected, premature, and deeply
regrettable, but it does not give us a sense of man's greatness achieved through understanding the sufferings that a
sufferer has at least in some degree chosen. Probably critics
hoard the term "tragedy" because it is also a word of praise:
to call a play a comedy or a problem play is not to imply anything about its merits, but to call a play a tragedy is tanta-
mount to calling it an important or even a great play. In
most of the best-known Greek tragedies the protagonist either
does some terrible deed or resists mightily. But Greek drama
has its pathetic figures too, figures who do not so much act
as suffer. Euripides's *The Trojan Women* is perhaps the greatest example of a play which does not allow its heroes to
choose and to act but only to undergo, to be in agony. When
we think of pathetic figures in Greek drama, however, we
probably think chiefly of the choruses, groups of rather commonplace persons who do not perform a tragic deed but who
suffer in sympathy with the tragic hero, who lament the hard-
ness of the times, and who draw the spectators into the range
of the hero's suffering.

Arthur Miller has argued that because Oedipus has given his name to a complex that the common man may have, the common man is therefore "as apt a subject for tragedy." It is not Oedipus's "complex," however, but his unique importance that is the issue in the play. Moreover, even if one argues that a man of no public importance may suffer as much as a man of public importance (and surely no one doubts this), one may be faced with the fact that the unimportant man by his ordinariness is not particularly good material for drama, and we are here concerned with drama rather than with life. In *Death of a Salesman* Willy Loman's wife says, rightly, "A small man can be just as exhausted as a great man." Yes, but is his exhaustion itself interesting, and do his activities (and this includes the words he utters) before his exhaustion have interesting dramatic possibilities? Isn't there a colorlessness that may weaken the play, an impoverishment of what John Milton called "gorgeous tragedy"?

Miller accurately noted (*Theatre Arts*, October 1953) that American drama "has been a steady year by year documentation of the frustration of man," and it is evident that Miller has set out to restore a sense of importance if not greatness to the individual. In "Tragedy and the Common Man," published in *The New York Times* (27 February 1949, sec. 2, pp. 1, 3) in the same year that *Death of a Salesman* was produced and evidently a defense of the play, he argues on behalf of the common man as a tragic figure and he insists that tragedy and pathos are very different: "Pathos truly is the mode of the pessimist. . . . The plays we revere, century after century, are the tragedies. In them, and in them alone, lies the belief — optimistic, if you will — in the perfectibility of man." Elsewhere (*Harper's*, August 1958) he has said that pathos is an oversimplification and therefore is the "counterfeit of meaning." Curiously, however, many spectators and readers find that by Miller's own terms Willy Loman fails to be a tragic figure; he seems to them pathetic rather than tragic, a victim rather than a man who acts and who wins our esteem. True, he is partly the victim of his own actions (although he could have chosen to be a carpenter, he chose to live by the bourgeois code that values a white collar), but he seems in larger part to be a victim of the system itself, a system of ruthless competition that has no place for the man who can no longer produce. (Here is an echo of the social-realist drama of the thirties.) Willy had believed in this system; and although his son Biff comes to the realization that Willy "had the wrong dreams," Willy himself seems not to achieve this insight. Of course he knows that he is out of a job, that the system does not value him any longer, but he still seems not to question the values he had subscribed to. Even in the last

minutes of the play, when he is planning his suicide in order
to provide money for his family -- really for Biff -- he says
such things as "Can you imagine his magnificence with twenty
thousand dollars in his pocket?" and "When the mail comes
he'll be ahead of Bernard again." In the preface to his
Collected Plays Miller comments on the "exultation" with which
Willy faces the end, but it is questionable whether an audience
shares it. Many people find that despite the gulf in rank,
they can share King Lear's feelings more easily than Willy's.

Suggested references: Several reviews and essays are collected
in *Two Modern American Tragedies*, John D. Hurrell, ed. (1961).
Among the reviews are pieces by Eleanor Clark (hostile), in
Partisan Review 26 (June 1949), pp. 631-35, and Harold Clurman
(favorable) in Clurman's *Lies Like Truth*. Hurrell also reprints
(from *Tulane Drama Review* 2 [May 1958], pp. 63-69) an interesting discussion between Miller and several critics.

Peter Shaffer, *Equus*. (The following discussion is an abridgement of an afterword in our *Types of Drama: Plays and Essays*,
3rd edition.) It is a commonplace of dramatic criticism that
Oedipus is a sort of detective story in which the detective,
Oedipus, searches for the criminal and discovers that he himself is the object of his search. Part of the greatness of
the play surely resides in the fact that Oedipus, in his relentless search for the truth, strips away all comforting
illusions, pursuing his quest even when it becomes evident
that he himself may be the culprit. Oedipus's triumph, and,
in part, ours as we watch him, is that he is determined to
know the truth at whatever cost.

In some ways, Peter Shaffer's *Equus*, too, is a sort of detective story. We are told at the start of the play that Alan
Strang has blinded six horses. As the play progresses, we
learn, through the psychiatrist's careful analytic or detective work, why Alan blinded the horses. The analyst uses the
devices of a detective: for example, he invites himself to the
boy's home to see what he can learn, and he does so on a Sunday: "If there's any tension over religion, it should be evident on a Sabbath evening." And bit by bit the full story of
the crime is revealed. In Scene 6 we are told that Alan
screams something that sounds like "Ek," but not until Scene
14 is this puzzle explained, when Alan's father mentions that
he heard the boy say, "Equus my only begotten son." Similarly,
we first hear about Jill, very casually, in Scene 12, but not
until much later do we understand the part she played in Alan's
life.

The stage-set itself -- "tiers of seats in the fashion of a dissecting theatre" surrounding the place of action -- contributes to this sense that we are watching a detective find his way, like a surgeon, to the hidden disease or crime. Two other implications of the set are also significant: the tiers surround a square that "resembles a railed boxing ring," and it is here that the two chief characters, Alan Strang and Dr. Martin Dysart, slug it out; the set perhaps also suggests a sort of courtroom, with Alan as both the witness and the criminal at the bar. The whole set, the square embraced by tiers on which spectators sit, is itself a sort of entire theater with actors and audience, but those of us who are spectators in the auditorium are linked to the action by means of our fellow spectators who, like the audience in a Greek amphitheater, sit in the tiers. We are onlookers, but insofar as we are aware of the spectators in the tiers we are looking at people like ourselves, and all of us are looking at a boy who had "always been such a gentle boy," and who had seemed, to the owner of the stable, an ideal stable-hand. We are watching, then, the uncovering of the deepest feelings that reside in what seems -- or had seemed -- to be a fairly ordinary boy.

But of course Alan is not a fairly ordinary boy; he had only seemed to be one. Although it is risky enough even for experts to try to psychoanalyze real people, and it is usually foolish to try to psychoanalyze characters in a play, it seems fairly clear that Alan is schizoid. That is, he has markedly withdrawn from reality. As the play progresses, we come to see that Alan, like the classic schizophrenic -- at least as understood by R. D. Laing in *The Politics of Experience* (1967) -- allows his outer self to live in the normal world (Alan lives a humdrum life at home and in the electrical supply store) but preserves an inner self that is radically contemptuous of the normal world and that sometimes suddenly shows itself in some violent, unsocial action. The inner life of such a person is more "real" than the outer, daily bodily life, and so Alan can insist to his god Equus, after the abortive sexual episode with Jill, "It wasn't me. Not really me." This is not mere weaseling; for the schizophrenic, there is a sharp separation between the real, inner "me" and the body that goes through a daily hateful routine.

For Alan, the horse is, among other things, an escape from the father and the dull world he represents ("Come on, Trojan -- bear me away"). "All that power going any way you wanted," and "Then suddenly I was on the ground where Dad pulled me. I could have bashed him." Moreover, the horse is the god Alan worships. This worship is filled with echoes from the Bible,

120

especially with suggestions of Christ. Equus, "born in the straw," is "in chains" for "the sins of the world"; when Alan takes Nugget out of the stable, he gives the horse a lump of sugar which is "His last supper"; when the horse eats the sugar he takes upon himself Alan's "sins," and Alan says, "Into my hands he commends himself,"echoing Jesus' words in Luke 23:46. "Father, into thy hands I commend my spirit." And Alan, fascinated by Nugget's eyes, believes Nugget sees everything, because Alan's mother had said, "God sees you, Alan. God's got eyes everywhere."

Any comments of what a play is "about" must, of course, be imprecise, for a play consists of thousands of details that inevitably make any summary and brief interpretation a distortion. Still, we can say that the play dramatizes not a curious case history but the tragic conflict between the world of passion and mystery and the world of numbness and sociability. Your students may have seen glimpses of some such conflict in another tragedy: Oedipus's passionate desire to find out the truth about his origins, versus Jocasta's sensible suggestion that it is best to let sleeping dogs lie; or Hamlet's passion versus Horatio's stoicism. The paradox in this play is that Dysart, the apparently rational psychiatrist who is charged with restoring Alan to the normal world, envies Alan's irrationality. It is Dysart's fate to be married to a dentist, a thoroughly sensible Scottish woman who cannot share his interest in the world of ancient art and ritual:

> I pass her a picture of the sacred acrobats of Crete leaping through the horns of running bulls -- and she'll say: "Och, Martin, what an *absurred* thing to be doing! The Highland Games, now there's a *normal sport!*" Or she'll observe, just after I've told her a story from the Iliad: "You know, when you come to think of it, Agamemnon and that lot were nothing but a bunch of ruffians from the Gorbals, only with fancy names!" You get the picture. She's turned into a Shrink.

But what of Dysart himself? Is he an Alan who has somehow bridged the gulf and managed to live a socially useful life? First of all, as he knows, he has none of Alan's passion. His trips to Greece are not "wild returns . . . to the womb of civilization":

> Three weeks a year in the Peleponnese, every bed booked in advance, every meal paid for by vouchers, cautious jaunts in hired Fiats, suitcase crammed with Kao-Pectate! Such a fantastic surrender to

121

the primitive. And I use that word endlessly: "primitive." "Oh, the primitive world," I say. "What instinctual truths were lost with it!" . . . I sit looking at pages of centaurs trampling the soil of Argos -- and outside my window he is trying to *become one*, in a Hampshire field!

Dysart's awareness of his own lack of deep feeling and of separation from mystery makes him envy Alan, particularly Alan's pain. "His pain. His own. He made it." It is a curious fact that as we look at the sufferings of tragic characters -- Oedipus insisting on an agonizing search for the truth that culminates when he blinds himself -- we feel that these sufferings are, in a way, their most precious possession. Lesser people are numbed by sufferings, but by taking on sufferings tragic heroes somehow fulfill themselves. They choose their way of life, and all that it entails. With Melville's Ahab they say, "Oh, now I feel my topmost greatness in my topmost grief." Some such awareness causes Dysart to say, "That boy has known a passion more ferocious than I have felt in any second of my life. And let me tell you something: I envy it." He has been critical of his way, and he goes on to dissect his own failure:

> The finicky, critical husband looking through his art books on mythical Greece. What worship has *he* ever known? Real worship! Without worship you shrink, it's as brutal as that . . . I shrank my own life.

If Alan's tragedy is that he has chosen a life radically different from the normal world's, and he must suffer for it, Dysart's is that he chose the normal world, and he suffers -- though less intensely -- from the knowledge that he has made the wrong choice. Even at the start of the play we heard suggestions to this effect. Dysart tells us that he is

> all reined up in old language and old assumptions, straining to jump clean-hoofed on to a whole new track of being I only suspect is there. I can't see it, because my educated, average head is being held at the wrong angle. I can't jump because the bit forbids it, and my own basic force -- my horsepower, if you like -- is too little. The only thing I know for sure is this: a horse's head is finally unknowable to me. Yet I handle children's heads -- which I must presume to be more complicated, at least in the area of my chief concern. . . . In a way, it has nothing to do with this boy. The doubts have been there for years, piling up steadily in

> this dreary place. It's only the extremity of this
> case that's made them active. I know that. The
> *extremity* is the point.

Tragic heroes thrive on "extremity," situations in which all
of the normal responses, all of the world's good sense, prove
to be inadequate, or at least are found to be inadequate by
the passionate individual who cannot let well enough alone,
who cannot go along with the way of the world. We can think
of Oedipus's determination to learn of his parentage, or of
Hamlet's determination to hear the Ghost's message, or even
Nora's determination to become a person.

Dysart clearly sees himself as one who does go the way of the
world, as one who is unwilling, or unable, to lay down his
life in order to achieve his personal dignity. His job is to
make people normal, to make healthy the sick, but he has come
to feel that he is the "priest" of the "murderous God of
Health." On the first night after he meets Alan he dreams
that he sacrifices children to the "normal," but he cannot
bring himself to sacrifice himself to his new insight. On the
other hand, Alan, superficially a most unlikely tragic hero,
rides with the god Equus against the world of the normal,
against "The Hosts of Hoover. The Hosts of Philco. . . . The
House of Remington and all its tribe." It is Dysart's job to
reconcile Alan to the normal world that Dysart scorns and yet
participates in. It is, in short, Dysart's sickening job to
deprive Alan of the worship of Equus. "Can you think of anything worse one can do to anybody than to take away their
worship?" Or to take away the pain by which a worshipper
knows he has preserved himself from the deadly claims of a
normal, socialized world? Dysart may be able to cure Alan
of his worship of Equus, but only at the cost of robbing Alan
of his most precious possession. "If you knew anything, you'd
get up this minute and run from me as fast as you could. . . .
My desire might be to make this boy an ardent husband -- a
caring citizen -- a worshipper of abstract and unifying God.
My achievement, however, is more likely to make a ghost." If
we have read *Oedipus*, we are familiar with a vision that shows
greatness finding itself in a painful sacrifice of self. And
this sacrifice somehow purifies or strengthens the society that
survives it. In *Equus*, Shaffer suggests that the sacrifice of
the deeply feeling hero brings not new strength or health to
society but only death, or death in life, for it represents
only the triumph of the normal.

A few words must be said about the nudity in Scene 33 because
it has provoked much comment. Surely, however, one thing it
does not provoke is any erotic feeling. It is not strictly

necessary, since in an earlier scene Alan simply mimes taking off his clothes, but it is entirely justifiable theatrically. In a way, it is foreshadowed in Scene 23, when Dysart explains to Alan's mother that the boy is "at a most delicate stage of treatment! He's totally exposed." And so in Scene 33, when Alan, reliving the sexual episode with Jill, collapses under the stress of his betrayal and failure, it is not only literally appropriate but also symbolically appropriate for him to be utterly naked, utterly vulnerable. As Brecht says, much tragic drama is a sort of striptease in which an individual's "innermost being is . . . driven into the open," and Shaffer has only made explicit and theatrical what is implicit. If the device has a fault, it is not that it is obscene but that it may embarrass an audience.

For a long discussion arguing that the play disguises a homosexual subject, see John Simon in *Hudson Review* 28, No. 1 (Spring 1975), pp. 97–106.

21

SOME OBSERVATIONS ON FILM

Anyone who pays attention to reviews of movies will have some ideas about what should and should not be said in talking about movies. The reviewers who interest us the most are Pauline Kael and John Simon, both of whom have published collections of their film criticism.

The one-volume history of the film that we find most useful is Gerald Mast's *A Short History of the Movies*; it covers a lot, but it also manages to give extended discussions of many films. Also valuable is Thomas Sobchack and Vivian C. Sobchack, *An Introduction to Film* (1980).

Other suggested titles, all especially relevant to literature:

> George Bluestone, *Novels into Film*
> John Harrington, *The Rhetoric of Film*
> James Hurt, ed., *Focus on Film and Theatre*
> William Jinks, *The Celluloid Literature: Film in the Humanities*
> James Monaco, *How to Read a Film*
> Fred H. Marcus, ed., *Film and Literature: Contrasts in Media*
> Gerald Mast, *The Comic Mind: Comedy and the Movies*
> Susan Sontag, *Against Interpretation*

And on films of Shakespeare:

> Charles W. Eckert, ed., *Focus on Shakespearean Films*
> Harry M. Geduld, *Filmguide to Henry V*
> Roger Manvell, *Shakespeare and the Film*

For a list of feature length sound films based on Shakespeare, with addresses of distributors, see *Shakespeare Newsletter* (November 1973), p. 44.

Appendix

WRITING ESSAYS ABOUT LITERATURE

Instructors who assign this chapter may want to know there is
a considerable body of published criticism on Frost's "Acquainted with the Night," centering chiefly on whether the
"luminary clock" in line 12 is a clock high on a building or
is the moon. Laurence Perrine, in *Explicator* 37 (Fall 1978),
pp. 13-14 summarizes many of the comments and reaffirms his
belief that the "luminary clock" is indeed a clock. Perrine
quotes sources who say that Frost said the clock was on a
building in Ann Arbor.

A THEMATIC TABLE OF CONTENTS TO
AN INTRODUCTION TO LITERATURE, SEVENTH EDITION

Most, but not all, of the selections in the book are listed
below; some are listed more than once. Selections are given
in the order they appear in the book.

127

THE CITY (cont'd)

Gwendolyn Brooks, We Real Cool

Lucille Clifton, in the inner city

Arthur Miller, Death of a Salesman

DEATH

Nathaniel Hawthorne, Roger Malvin's Burial

Leo Tolstoy, The Death of Ivan Ilych

Katherine Anne Porter, The Jilting of Granny Weatherall

Jean Rhys, I Used to Live Here Once

Shirley Jackson, The Lottery

Flannery O'Connor, A Good Man Is Hard to Find

Donald Barthelme, The School

Anonymous, Sir Patrick Spence

Anonymous, The Three Ravens

Anonymous, The Twa Corbies

Anonymous, Edward

Anonymous, The Demon Lover

Robert Frost, Stopping by Woods on a Snowy Evening

Gerard Manley Hopkins, Spring and Fall: To a Young Child

Emily Dickinson, Because I could not stop for Death

Randall Jarrell, The Death of the Ball Turret Gunner

Wallace Stevens, The Emperor of Ice-Cream

John Crowe Ransom, Bells for John Whiteside's Daughter

A. E. Housman, Eight O'Clock

William Shakespeare, Fear no more the heat o' th' sun

Dylan Thomas, Do not go gentle into that good night

William Shakespeare, Sonnet 73 (That time of year thou mayst in me behold)

Alfred, Lord Tennyson, Ulysses

Emily Dickinson, I heard a Fly buzz--when I died

Thomas Hardy, Ah, Are You Digging on My Grave?

Thomas Hardy, During Wind and Rain

A. E. Housman, Shropshire Lad #19 (To an Athlete Dying Young)

Edwin Arlington Robinson, Richard Cory

Edwin Arlington Robinson, Mr. Flood's Party

Robert Frost, Design

Theodore Roethke, Elegy for Jane

Robert Lowell, Mr. Edwards
and the Spider

John Millington Synge, Riders
to the Sea

William Shakespeare, Hamlet

Arthur Miller, Death of a
Salesman

FAITH, FAITH AND DOUBT

Ernest Hemingway, A Clean,
Well-Lighted Place

Nathaniel Hawthorne, Young
Goodman Brown

Nathaniel Hawthorne, Roger
Malvin's Burial

Leo Tolstoy, The Death of
Ivan Ilych

Katherine Anne Porter, The
Jilting of Granny Weatherall

Flannery O'Connor, Revelation

William Shakespeare, Sonnet
146 (Poor soul, the center
of my sinful earth)

George Herbert, The Pulley

John Donne, Holy Sonnet XIV
(Batter my heart, three-
personed God)

John Milton, When I consider
how my light is spent

Matthew Arnold, Dover Beach

Gerard Manley Hopkins, God's
Grandeur

Gerard Manley Hopkins, Spring

T. S. Eliot, Journey of the
Magi

Robert Lowell, Mr. Edwards
and the Spider

Anonymous, Quem Quaeritis

John Millington Synge,
Riders to the Sea

William Shakespeare, Hamlet

THE FAMILY

Nathaniel Hawthorne, Roger
Malvin's Burial

Leo Tolstoy, The Death of
Ivan Ilych

Franz Kafka, The Metamorphosis

William Faulkner, Barn
Burning

Eudora Welty, A Worn Path

Alice Walker, Everyday Use

Anonymous, Edward

Theodore Roethke, My Papa's
Waltz

Thomas Hardy, During Wind
and Rain

Robert Hayden, Those Winter
Sundays

Sylvia Plath, Daddy

THE FAMILY (cont'd)

Dona Stein, Putting Mother By

John Millington Synge, Riders to the Sea

Sophocles, Antigonê

Sophocles, Oedipus Rex

William Shakespeare, Hamlet

Henrik Ibsen, A Doll's House

Tennessee Williams, The Glass Menagerie

Arthur Miller, Death of a Salesman

Peter Shaffer, Equus

GOOD AND EVIL

Luke, Parable of the Good Samaritan

Frank O'Connor, Guests of the Nation

Nathaniel Hawthorne, Young Goodman Brown

Nathaniel Hawthorne, Roger Malvin's Burial

Leo Tolstoy, The Death of Ivan Ilych

William Faulkner, Barn Burning

Flannery O'Connor, A Good Man Is Hard to Find

Flannery O'Connor, Revelation

Joyce Carol Oates, Where Are You Going, Where Have You Been?

D. H. Lawrence, Snake

John Keats, La Belle Dame sans Merci

Emily Dickinson, A narrow Fellow in the Grass

William Butler Yeats, Leda and the Swan

Robert Lowell, Mr. Edwards and the Spider

Sophocles, Antigonê

Sophocles, Oedipus Rex

William Shakespeare, Hamlet

Henrik Ibsen, A Doll's House

Arthur Miller, Death of a Salesman

Peter Shaffer, Equus

IDEALISM

William Faulkner, The Bear

Ernest Hemingway, A Clean, Well-Lighted Place

Leo Tolstoy, The Death of Ivan Ilych

James Joyce, Araby

Flannery O'Connor, Revelation

Donald Barthelme, The School

Toni Cade Bambara, The Lesson

Walt Whitman, A Noiseless Patient Spider

John Keats, Ode on a Grecian Urn

John Keats, On First Looking into Chapman's Homer

Walt Whitman, When I Heard the Learn'd Astronomer

Alfred, Lord Tennyson, Ulysses

Walt Whitman, Out of the Cradle Endlessly Rocking

A. E. Housman, Shropshire Lad #19 (To an Athlete Dying Young)

Sophocles, Antigonê

Molière, The Misanthrope

William Shakespeare, Hamlet

Henrik Ibsen, A Doll's House

Tennessee Williams, The Glass Menagerie

Arthur Miller, Death of a Salesman

Peter Shaffer, Equus

ILLUSION AND REALITY

Frank O'Connor, Guests of the Nation

Nathaniel Hawthorne, Young Goodman Brown

Nathaniel Hawthorne, Roger Malvin's Burial

Leo Tolstoy, The Death of Ivan Ilych

James Joyce, Araby

Thomas Gray, Ode on the Death of a Favorite Cat Drowned in a Tub of Gold-Fishes

Samuel Taylor Coleridge, Kubla Khan

Percy Bysshe Shelley, Ozymandias

Thomas Hardy, The Convergence of the Twain

Molière, The Misanthrope

Sophocles, Oedipus Rex

William Shakespeare, Hamlet

Henrik Ibsen, A Doll's House

Tennessee Williams, The Glass Menagerie

Arthur Miller, Death of a Salesman

Peter Shaffer, Equus

THE INDIVIDUAL AND SOCIETY

Luke, Parable of the Good Samaritan

Frank O'Connor, Guests of the Nation

THE INDIVIDUAL AND SOCIETY
(cont'd)

Nathaniel Hawthorne, Young
Goodman Brown

Nathaniel Hawthorne, Roger
Malvin's Burial

Leo Tolstoy, The Death of
Ivan Ilych

Franz Kafka, The Metamorphosis

James Thurber, The Secret
Life of Walter Mitty

Ralph Ellison, King of the
Bingo Game

Shirley Jackson, The Lottery

Flannery O'Connor, Revelation

Toni Cade Bambara, The
Lesson

Anonymous, Sir Patrick
Spence

Robert Frost, Mending Wall

E. E. Cummings, next to of
course god america i

William Carlos Williams,
The Yachts

Stevie Smith, Not Waving but
Drowning

William Wordsworth, Composed
upon Westminster Bridge,
September 3, 1802

Edwin Arlington Robinson,
Mr. Flood's Party

T. S. Eliot, The Love Song
of J. Alfred Prufrock

W. H. Auden, The Unknown
Citizen

Randall Jarrell, The Woman
at the Washington Zoo

Don H. Lee, But He Was Cool
or: he even stopped for green
lights

Sophocles, Antigonê

Molière, The Misanthrope

William Shakespeare, Hamlet

Henrik Ibsen, A Doll's House

Tennessee Williams, The Glass
Menagerie

Arthur Miller, Death of a
Salesman

Peter Shaffer, Equus

Robert Frost, Acquainted
with the Night

INNOCENCE AND EXPERIENCE
(See also YOUTH)

Frank O'Connor, Guests of
the Nation

William Faulkner, The Bear

Nathaniel Hawthorne, Young
Goodman Brown

Leo Tolstoy, The Death of
Ivan Ilych

James Joyce, Araby

William Faulkner, Barn
Burning

Flannery O'Connor, Revelation

John Updike, A&P

Donald Barthelme, The School

Joyce Carol Oates, Where Are
You Going, Where Have You
Been?

Toni Cade Bambara, The Lesson

Gerard Manley Hopkins, Spring
and Fall: To a Young Child

John Keats, On First Looking
into Chapman's Homer

William Blake, The Lamb

William Blake, The Tyger

Robert Hayden, Those Winter
Sundays

Dylan Thomas, Fern Hill

Gary Snyder, Hay for the
Horses

Sophocles, Oedipus Rex

William Shakespeare, Hamlet

Henrik Ibsen, A Doll's House

Tennessee Williams, The Glass
Menagerie

Arthur Miller, Death of a
Salesman

Peter Shaffer, Equus

ISOLATION

Frank O'Connor, Guests of
the Nation

Ernest Hemingway, A Clean,
Well-Lighted Place

Nathaniel Hawthorne, Young
Goodman Brown

Nathaniel Hawthorne, Roger
Malvin's Burial

Leo Tolstoy, The Death of
Ivan Ilych

Charlotte Perkins Gilman,
The Yellow Wallpaper

James Joyce, Araby

Franz Kafka, The Metamorphosis

Katherine Anne Porter, The
Jilting of Granny Weatherall

James Thurber, The Secret
Life of Walter Mitty

William Faulkner, A Rose for
Emily

William Faulkner, Barn
Burning

John Lennon and Paul McCartney,
Eleanor Rigby

Anonymous, Western Wind

Langston Hughes, Evenin' Air
Blues

ISOLATION (cont'd)

Robert Frost, Stopping by Woods on a Snowy Evening

Matthew Arnold, Dover Beach

Edwin Arlington Robinson, Richard Corey

Edwin Arlington Robinson, Mr. Flood's Party

Robert Frost, The Wood-Pile

T. S. Eliot, The Love Song of J. Alfred Prufrock

T. S. Eliot, The Journey of the Magi

Randall Jarrell, The Woman at the Washington Zoo

Allen Ginsberg, A Supermarket in California

Nikki Giovanni, Master Charge Blues

Sophocles, Antigoné

Molière, The Misanthrope

Sophocles, Oedipus Rex

William Shakespeare, Hamlet

Tennessee Williams, The Glass Menagerie

Arthur Miller, Death of a Salesman

Peter Shaffer, Equus

Robert Frost, Acquainted with the Night

LOVE

Petronius, The Widow of Ephesus

Luke, Parable of the Prodigal Son

James Joyce, Araby

Franz Kafka, The Metamorphosis

D. H. Lawrence, The Horse Dealer's Daughter

Eudora Welty, A Worn Path

Katherine Anne Porter, The Jilting of Granny Weatherall

Anonymous, Western Wind

Emily Dickinson, Wild nights

Robert Burns, Mary Morison

Robert Burns, John Anderson My Jo

Robert Herrick, To the Virgins, to Make Much of Time

William Carlos Williams, This Is Just to Say

Michael Drayton, Since there's no help

John Crowe Ransom, Piazza Piece

Robert Burns, A Red, Red Rose

Edmund Waller, Song

Andrew Marvell, To His Coy Mistress

John Donne, The Flea

William Shakespeare, Sonnet 29 (When in disgrace)

William Shakespeare, Sonnet 73 (That time of year)

John Donne, A Valediction: Forbidding Mourning

Robert Herrick, Corinna's Going A-Maying

Robert Browning, Porphyria's Lover

Matthew Arnold, Dover Beach

T. S. Eliot, The Love Song of J. Alfred Prufrock

E. E. Cummings, anyone lived in a pretty how town

Theodore Roethke, Elegy for Jane

Adrienne Rich, Living in Sin

Seamus Heaney, The Skunk

Dona Stein, Putting Mother By

William Shakespeare, Hamlet

Henrik Ibsen, A Doll's House

Tennessee Williams, The Glass Menagerie

LOVE AND HATE

Kate Chopin, The Story of an Hour

Edgar Allan Poe, The Cask of Amontillado

Leo Tolstoy, The Death of Ivan Ilych

Charlotte Perkins Gilman, The Yellow Wallpaper

William Faulkner, A Rose for Emily

Flannery O'Connor, A Good Man Is Hard to Find

Flannery O'Connor, Revelation

Joyce Carol Oates, Where Are You Going, Where Have You Been?

Anonymous, The Twa Corbies

Anonymous, Edward

Anonymous, The Demon Lover

Robert Browning, My Last Duchess

William Blake, The Sick Rose

Robert Browning, Porphyria's Lover

Robert Browning, Soliloquy of a Spanish Cloister

Sylvia Plath, Daddy

Molière, The Misanthrope

William Shakespeare, Hamlet

Peter Shaffer, Equus

NATURE

William Faulkner,   The Bear

William Shakespeare,   When
daisies pied and violets blue

William Shakespeare,   When
icicles hang by the wall

Robert Frost,   Mending Wall

Gerard Manley Hopkins,   Spring
and Fall: To a Young Child

William Carlos Williams,   The
Yachts

Wallace Stevens,   Anecdote
of the Jar

D. H. Lawrence,   Snake

Robbert Herrick,   Corinna's
Going A-Maying

William Wordsworth,   Composed
upon Westminster Bridge,
September 3, 1802

William Wordsworth,   I
Wandered Lonely as a Cloud

John Keats,   To Autumn

Emily Dickinson,   A narrow
Fellow in the Grass

Gerard Manley Hopkins,   God's
Grandeur

Gerard Manley Hopkins,   Spring

A. E. Housman,   Loveliest of
trees, the cherry now

Robert Frost,   The Wood-Pile

William Carlos Williams,
Spring and All

Theodore Roethke,   Elegy for
Jane

Donald Hall,   Names of Horses

Dave Smith,   The Spring Poem

John Millington Synge,
Riders to the Sea

WAR

Frank O'Connor,   Guests of
the Nation

YOUTH
(See also INNOCENCE AND
EXPERIENCE)

Frank O'Connor,   Guests of
the Nation

William Faulkner,   The Bear

James Joyce,   Araby

William Faulkner,   Barn
Burning

Donald Barthelme,   The School

Joyce Carol Oates,   Where Are
You Going, Where Have You
Been?

Toni Cade Bambara,   The Lesson

Gerard Manley Hopkins,   Spring
and Fall: To a Young Child

John Updike,   Youth's Progress

Gwendolyn Brooks, We Real
Cool

Peter Shaffer, Equus